Sugar Skulls

Coloring Book

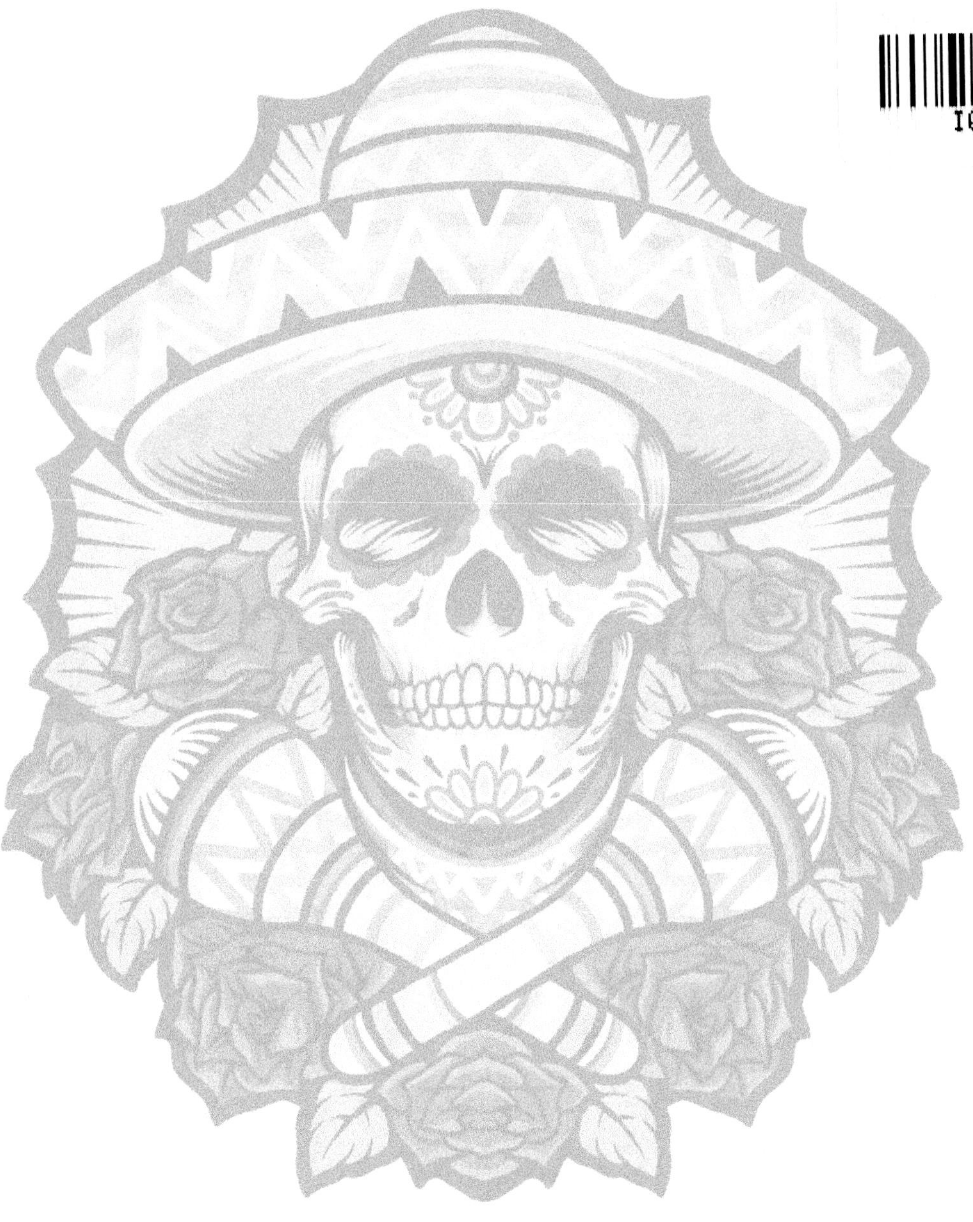

I0491957

FOR ADULT & TEEN

This book

belongs to

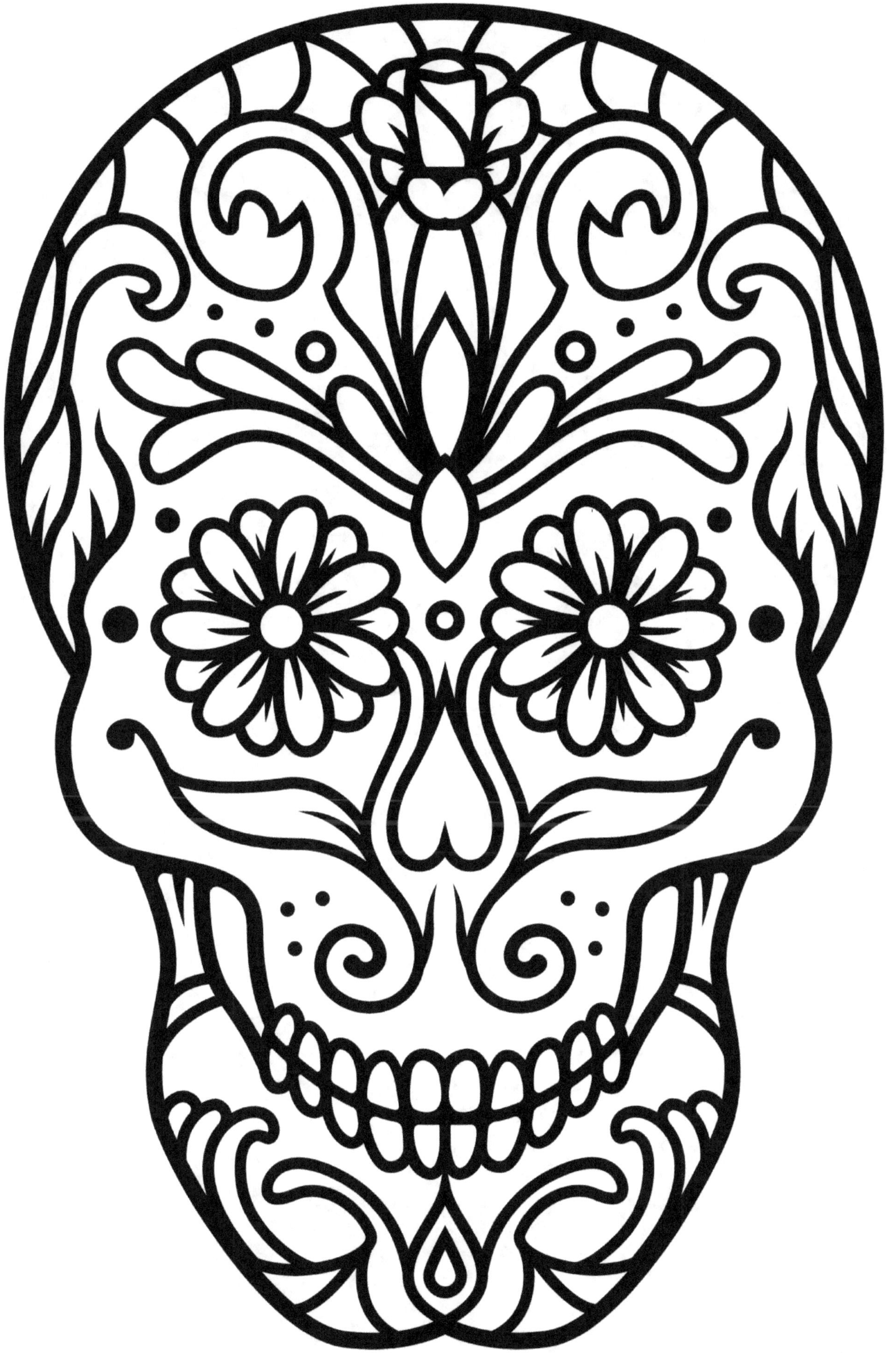

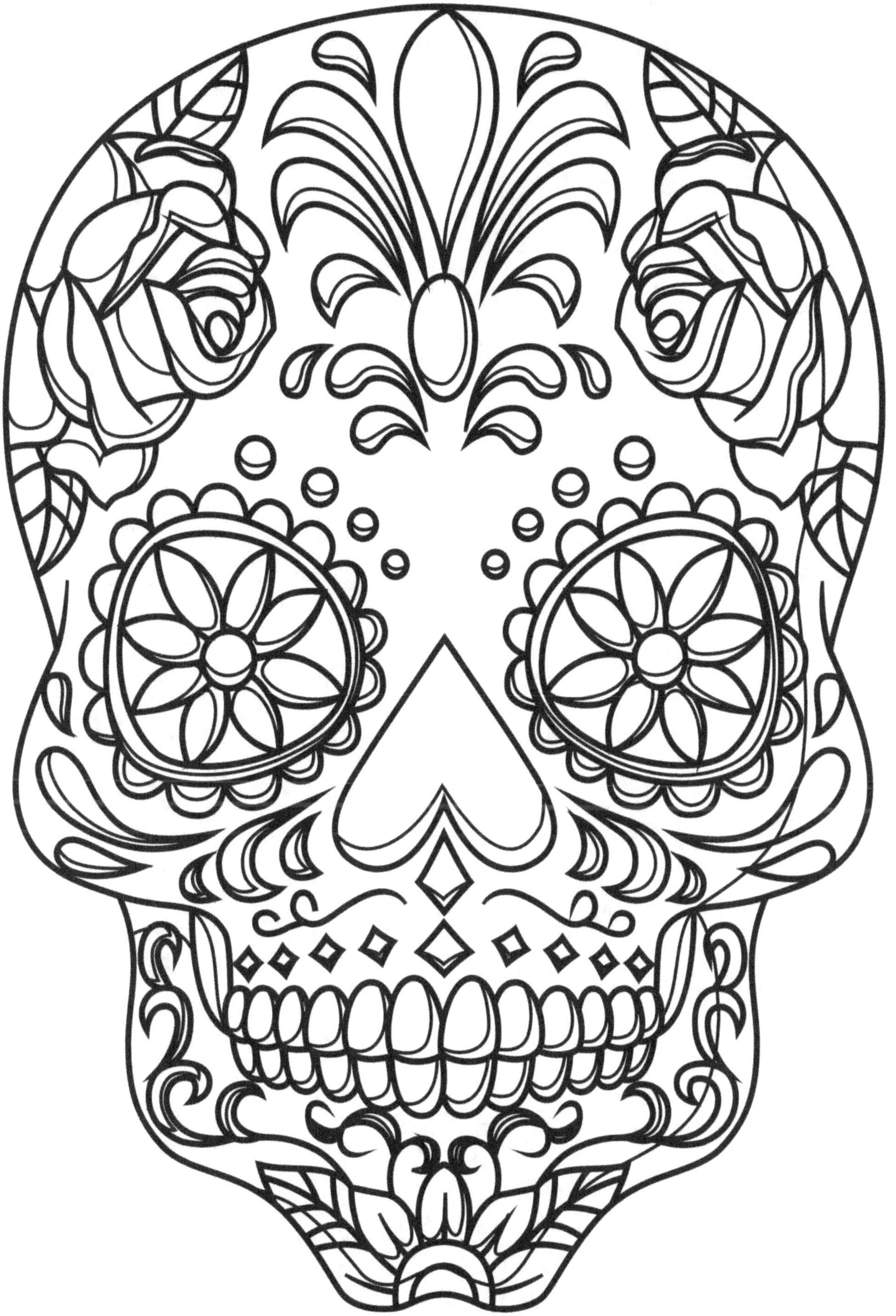

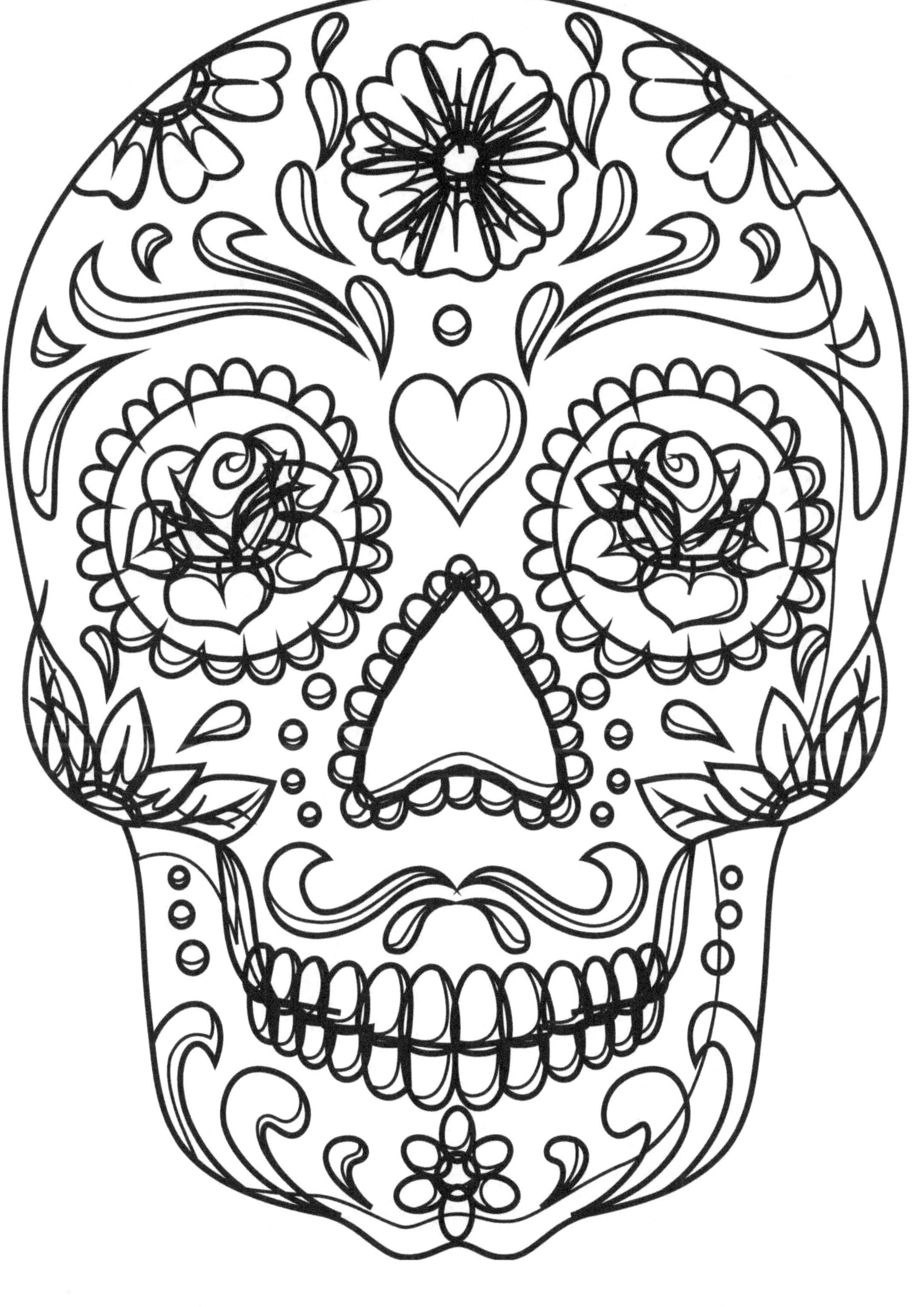

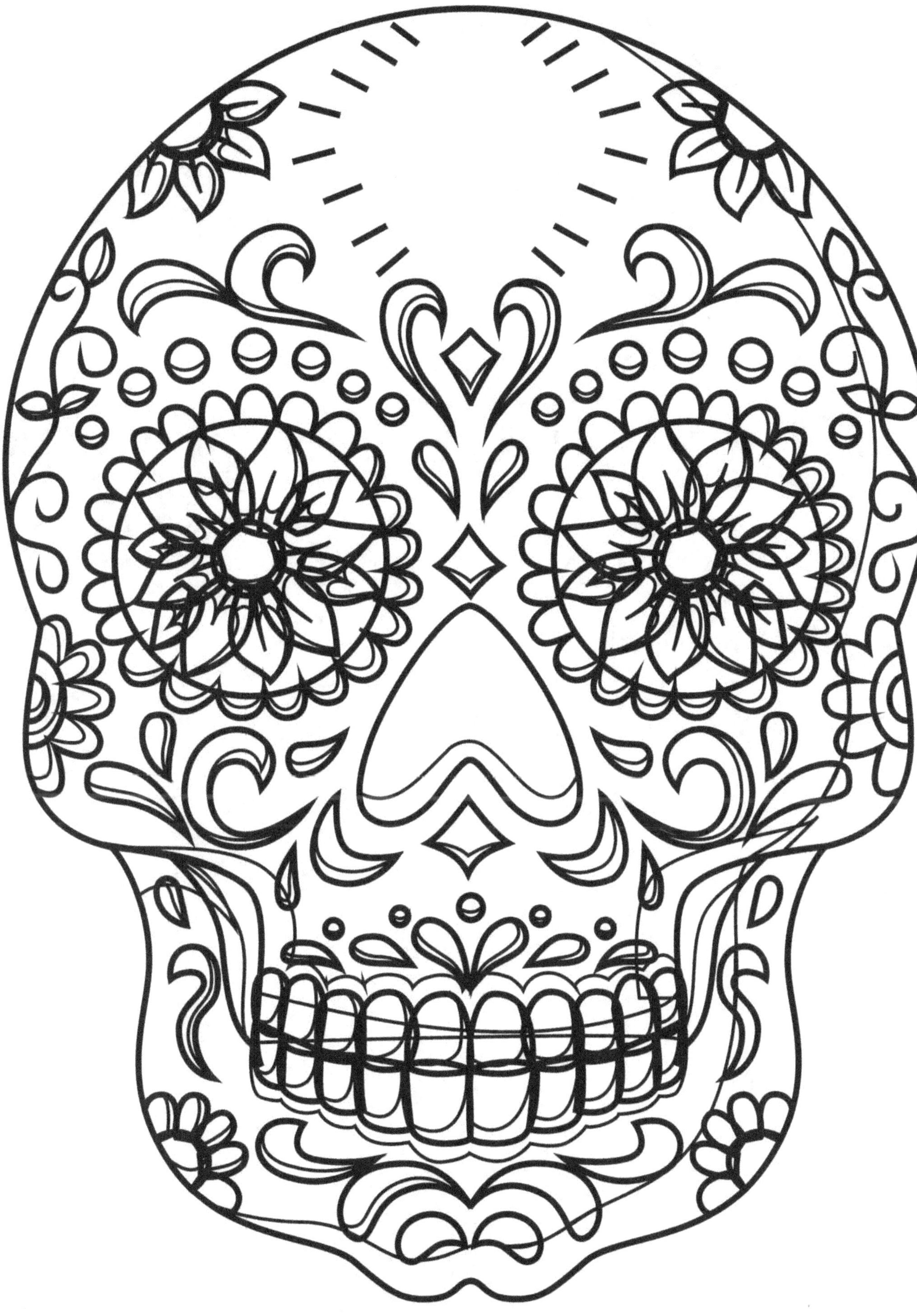

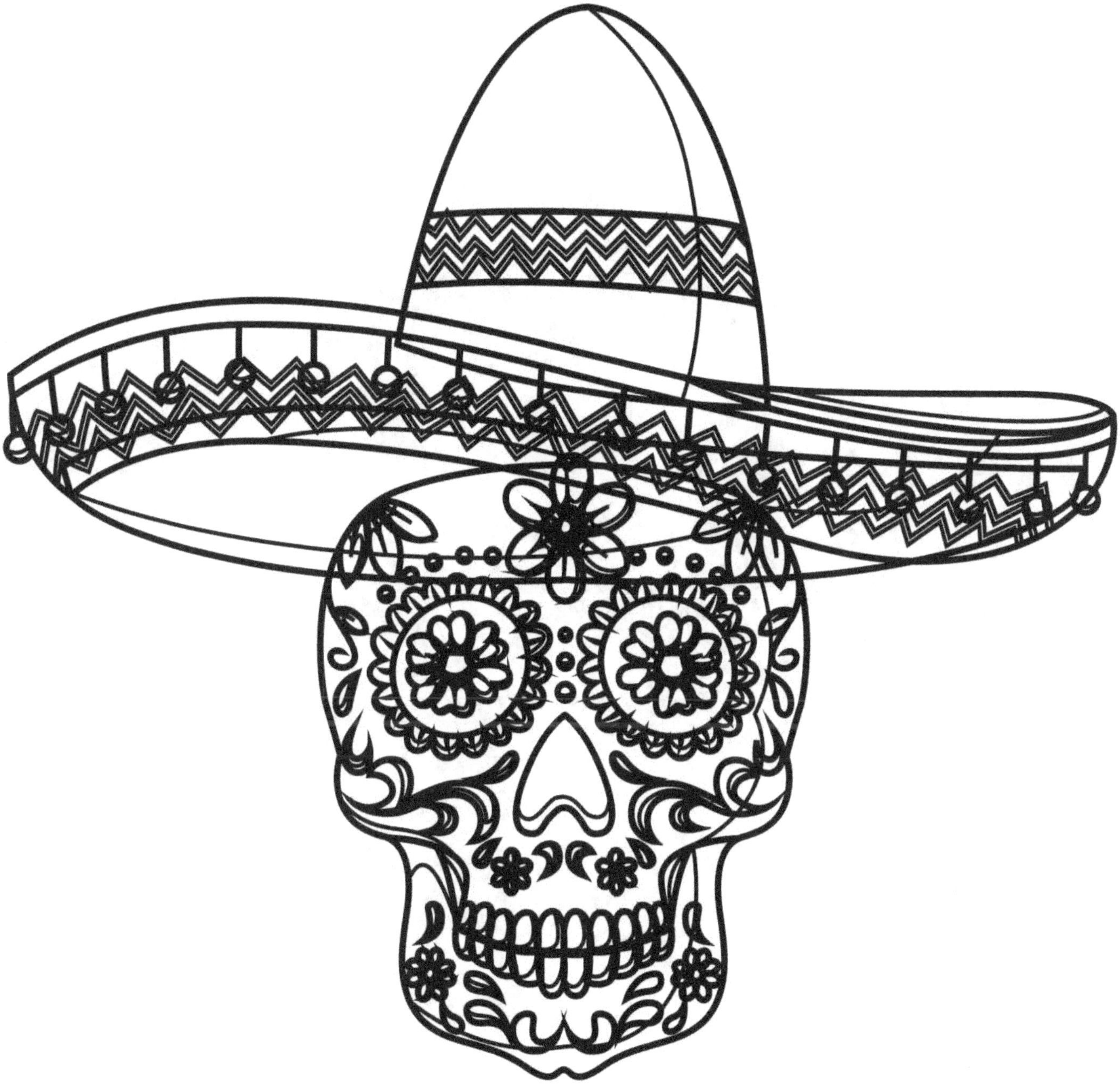

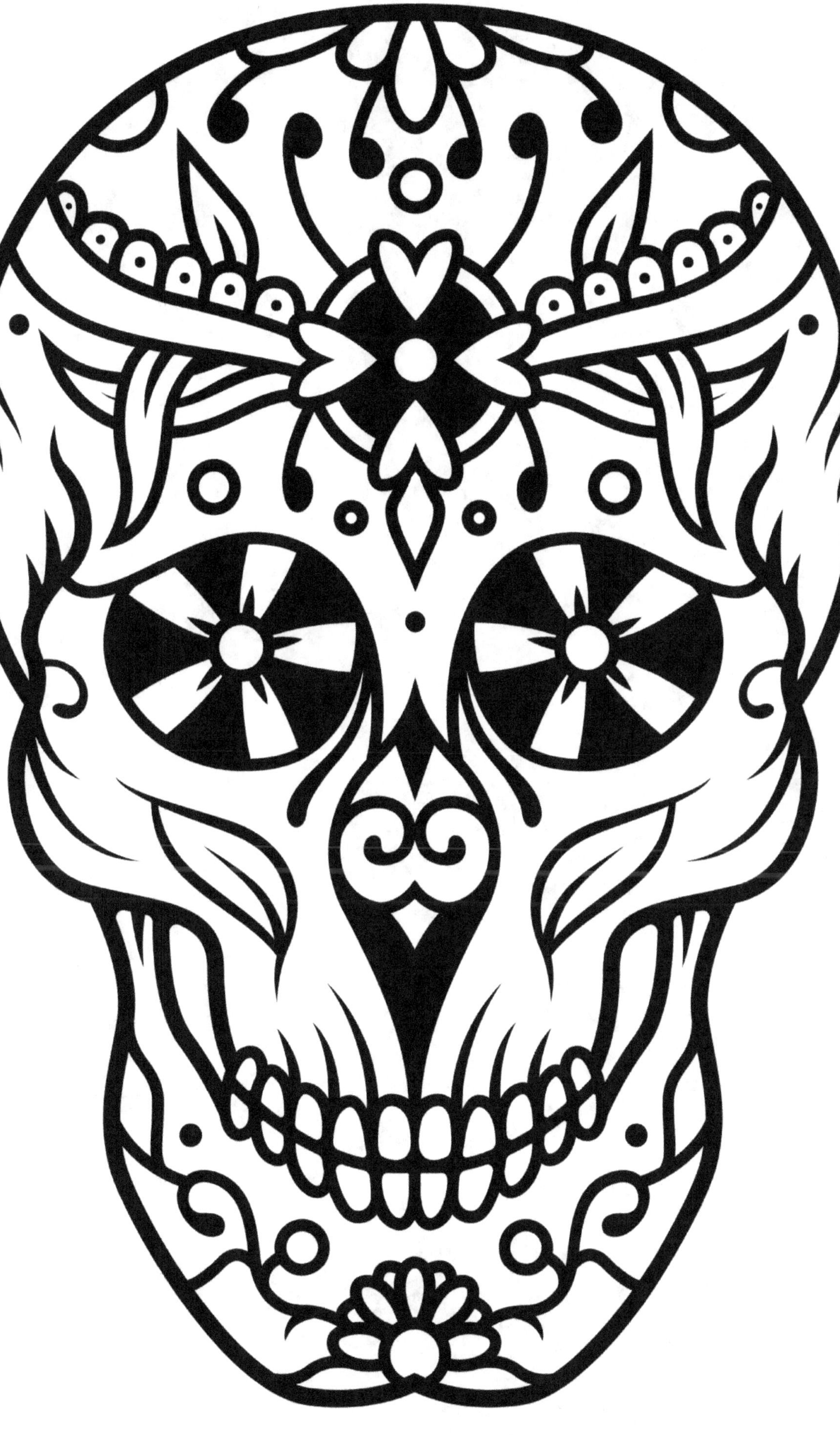

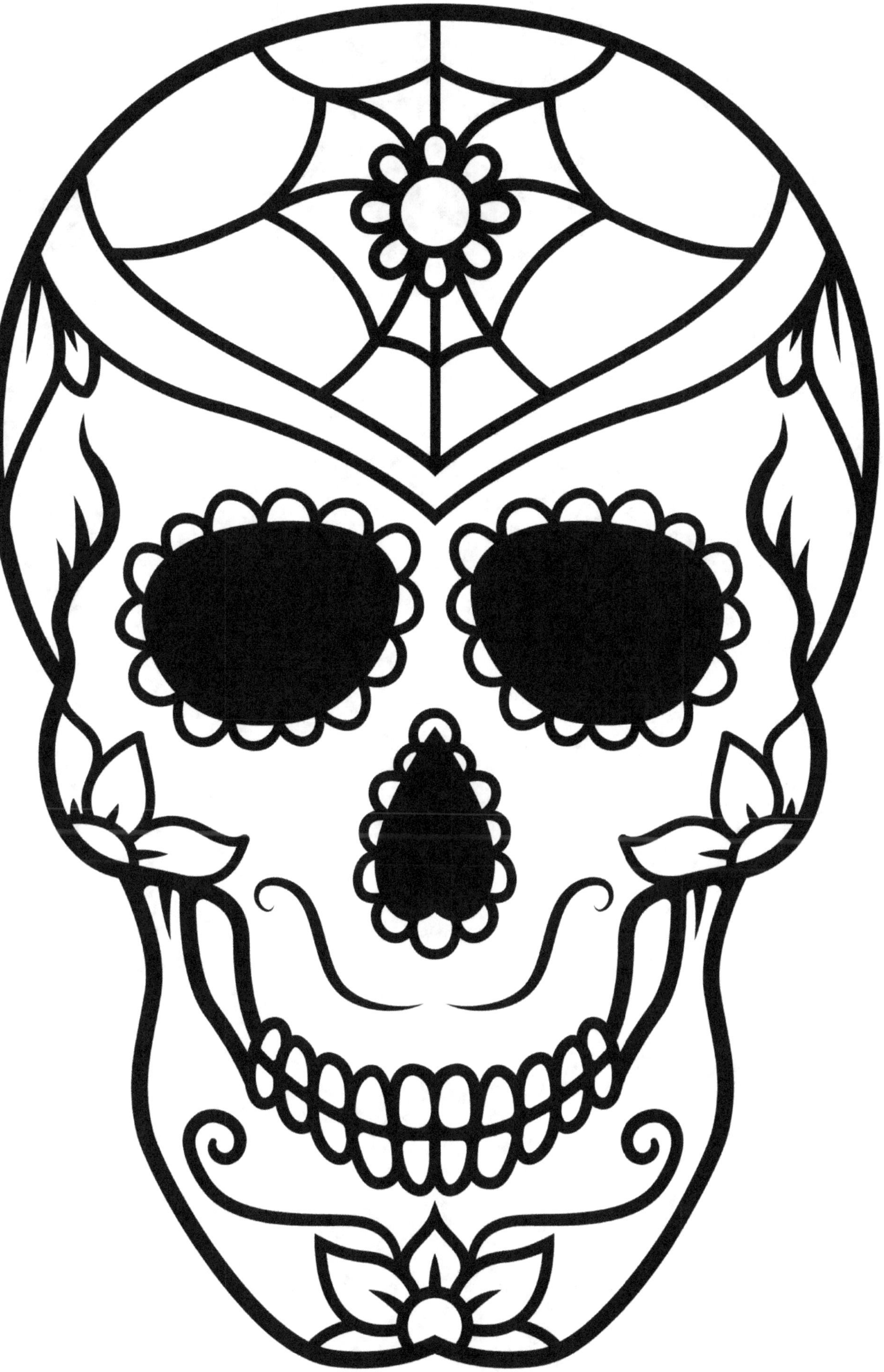

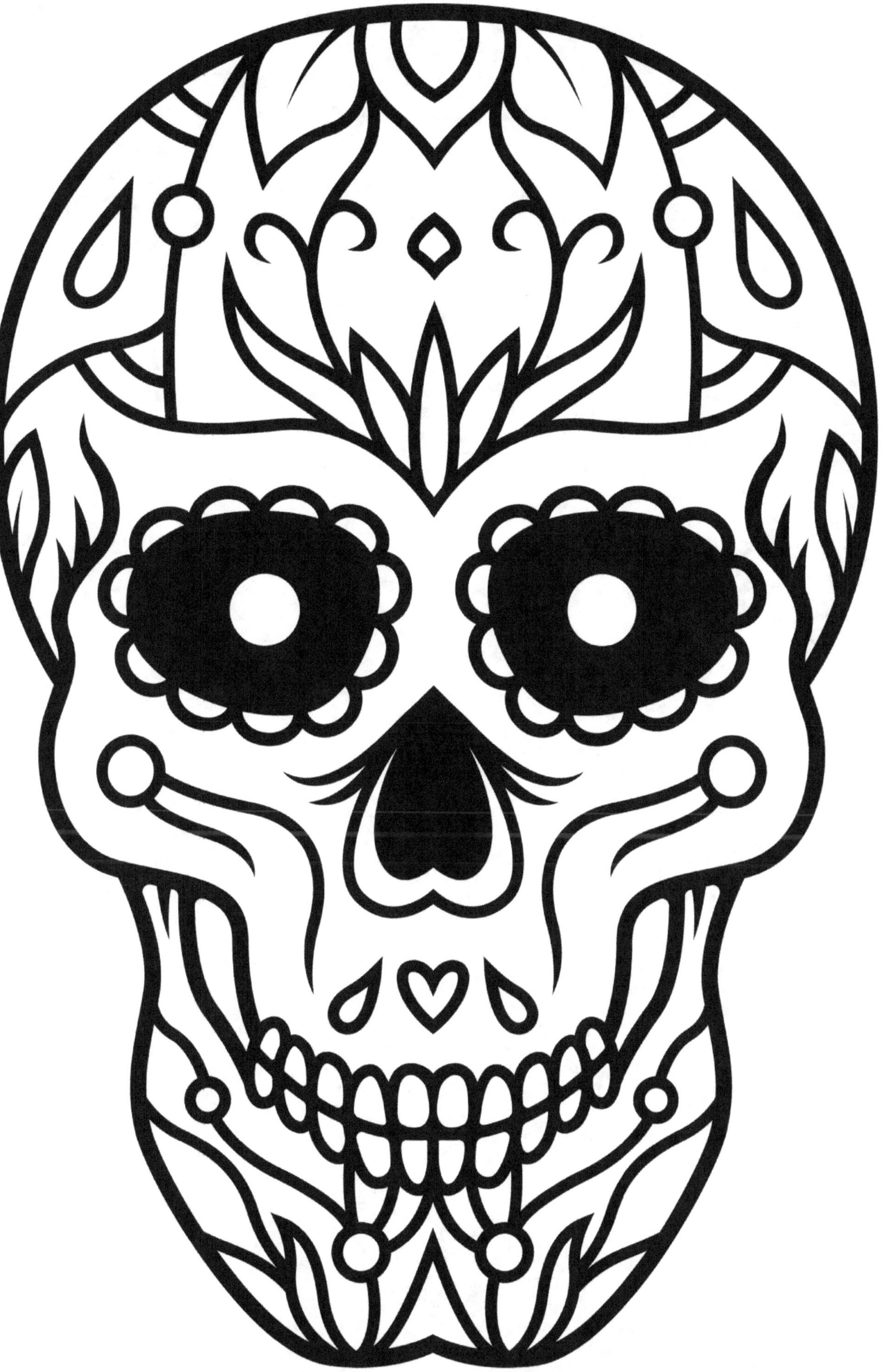

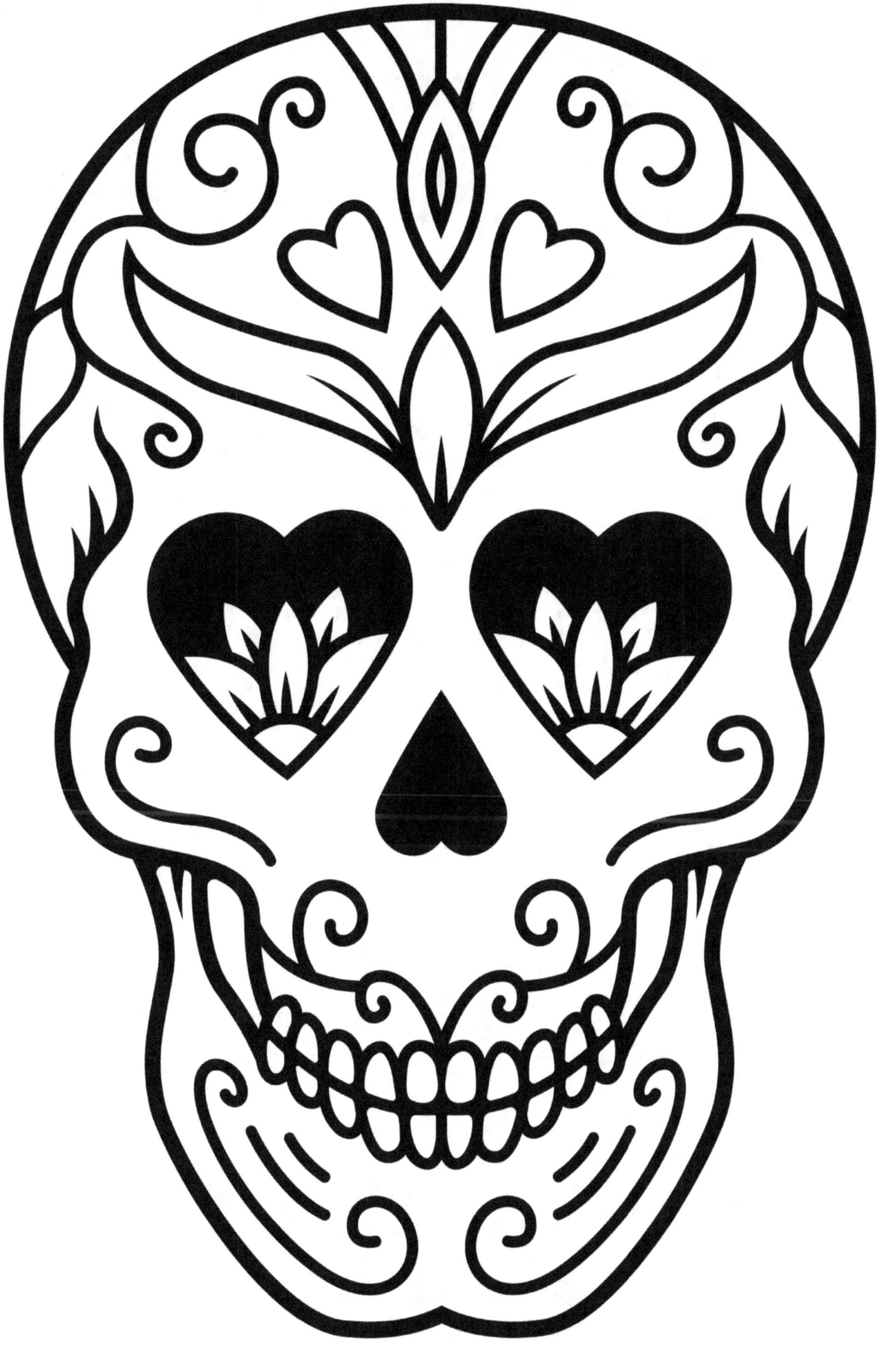

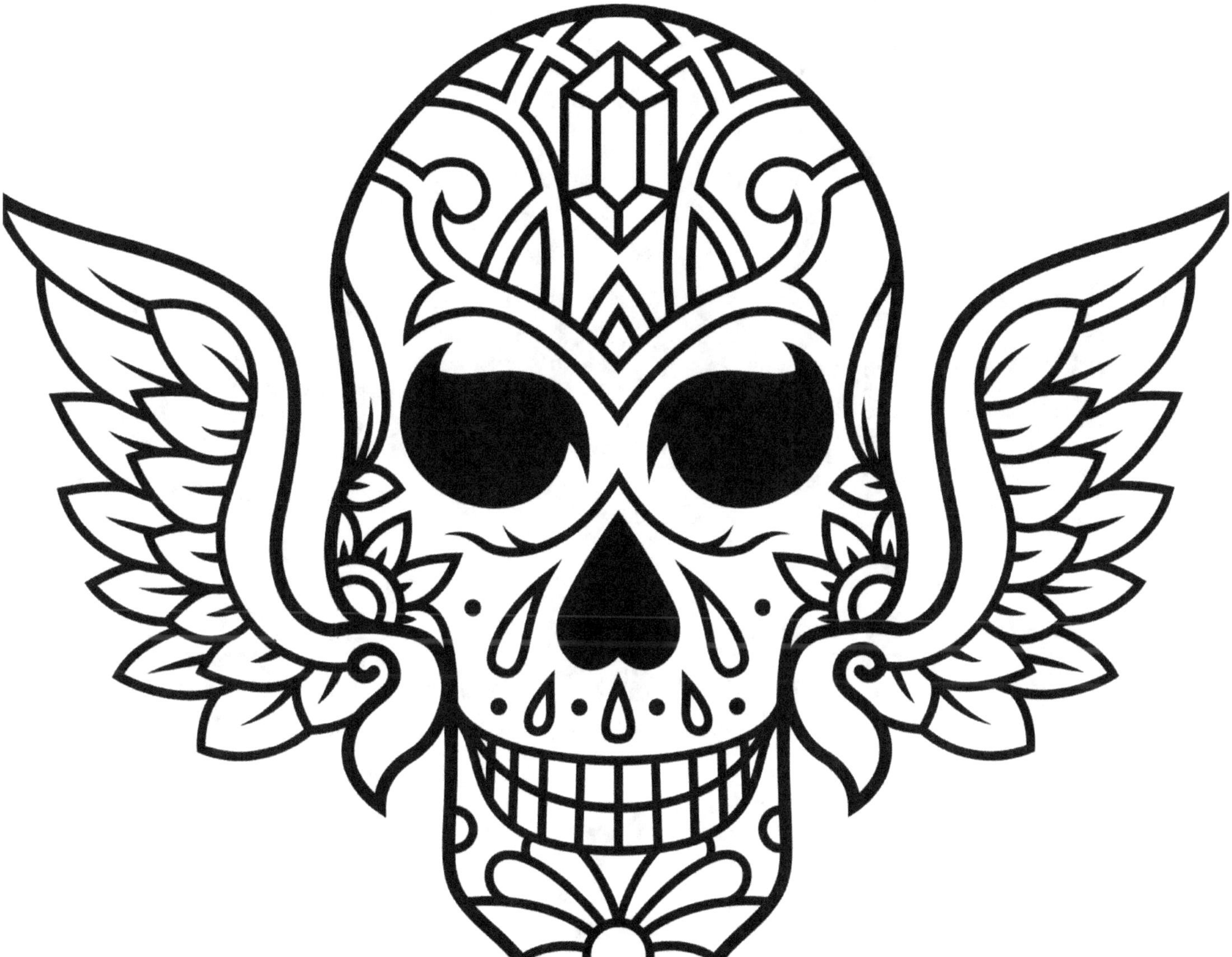

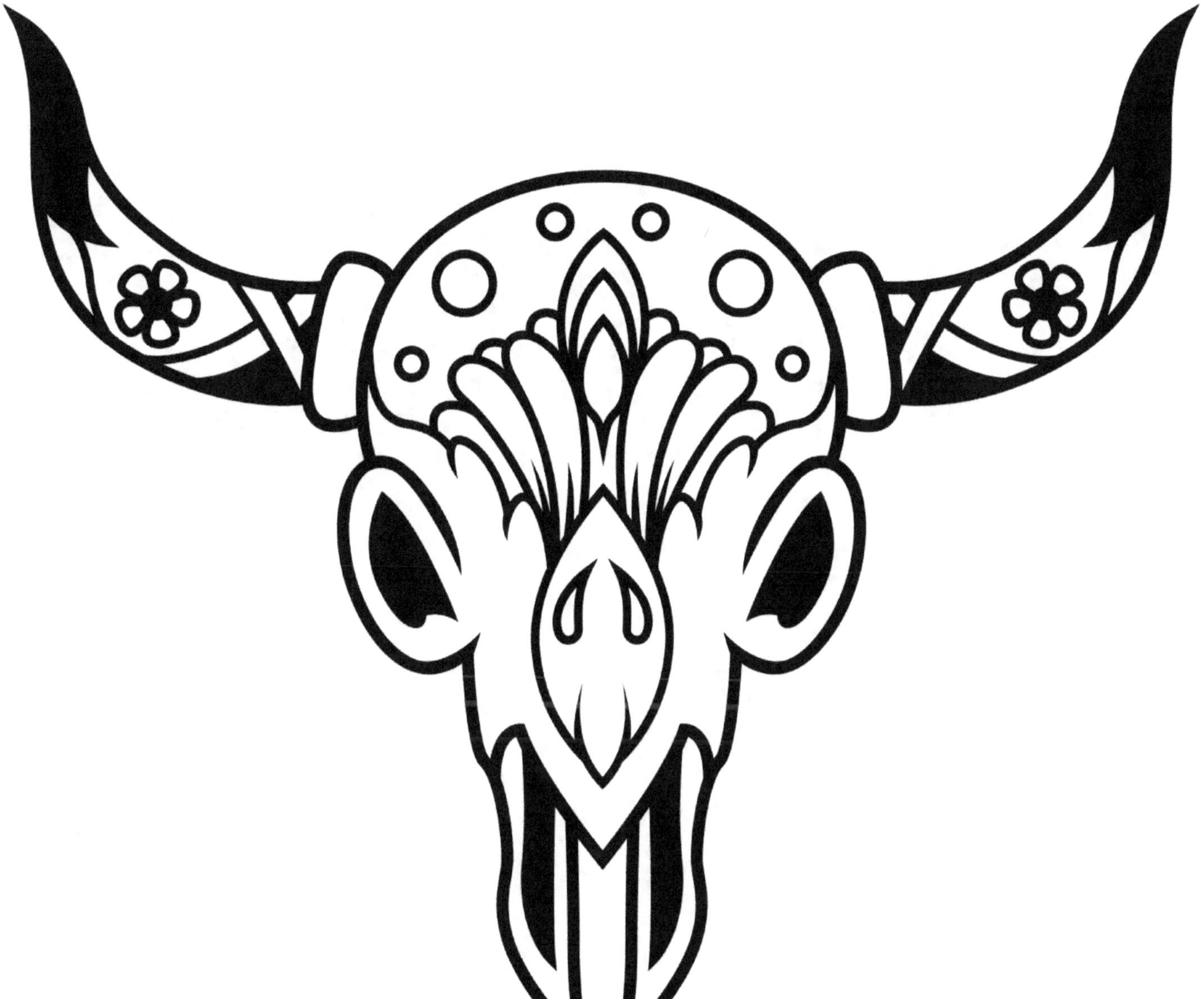

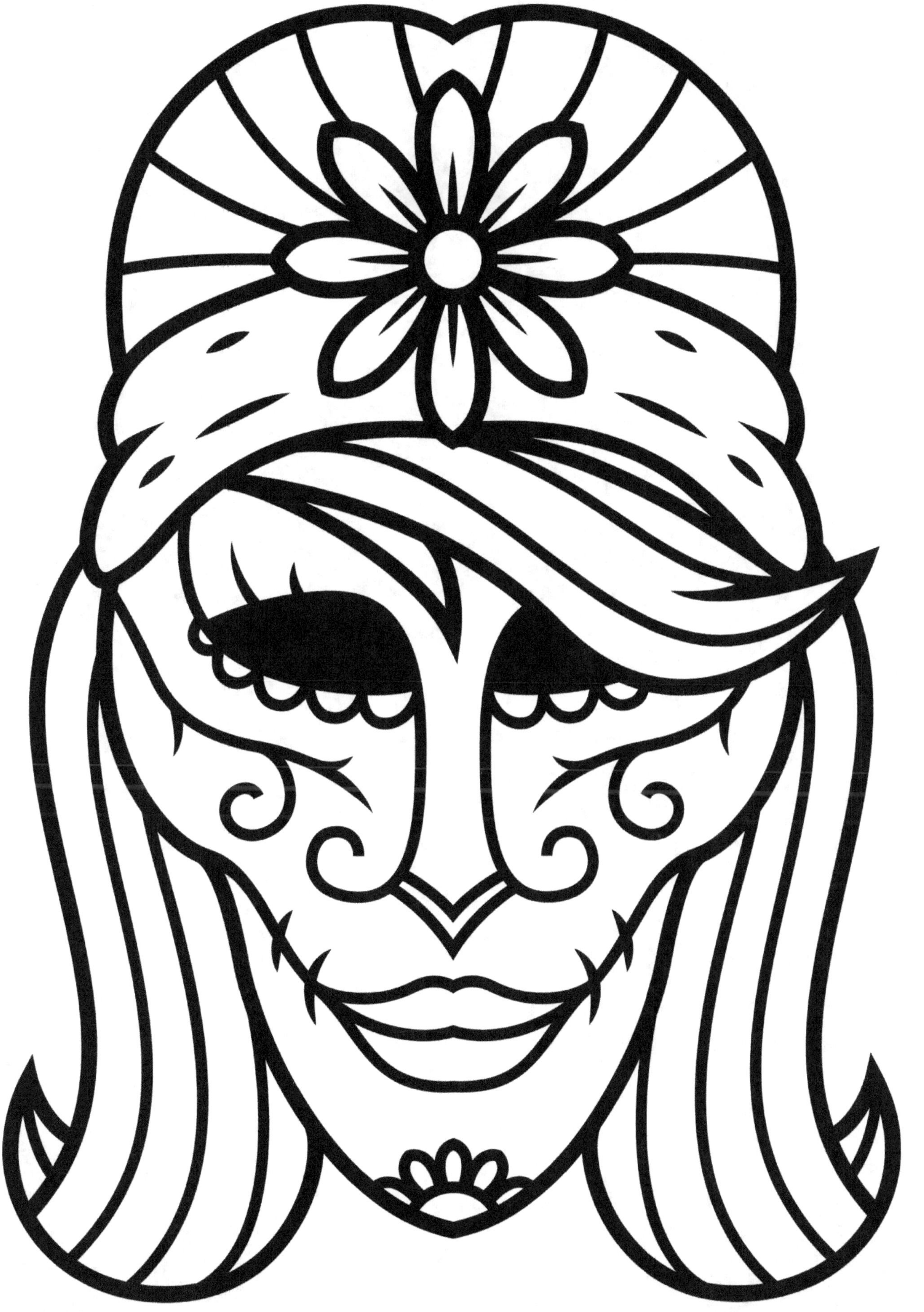

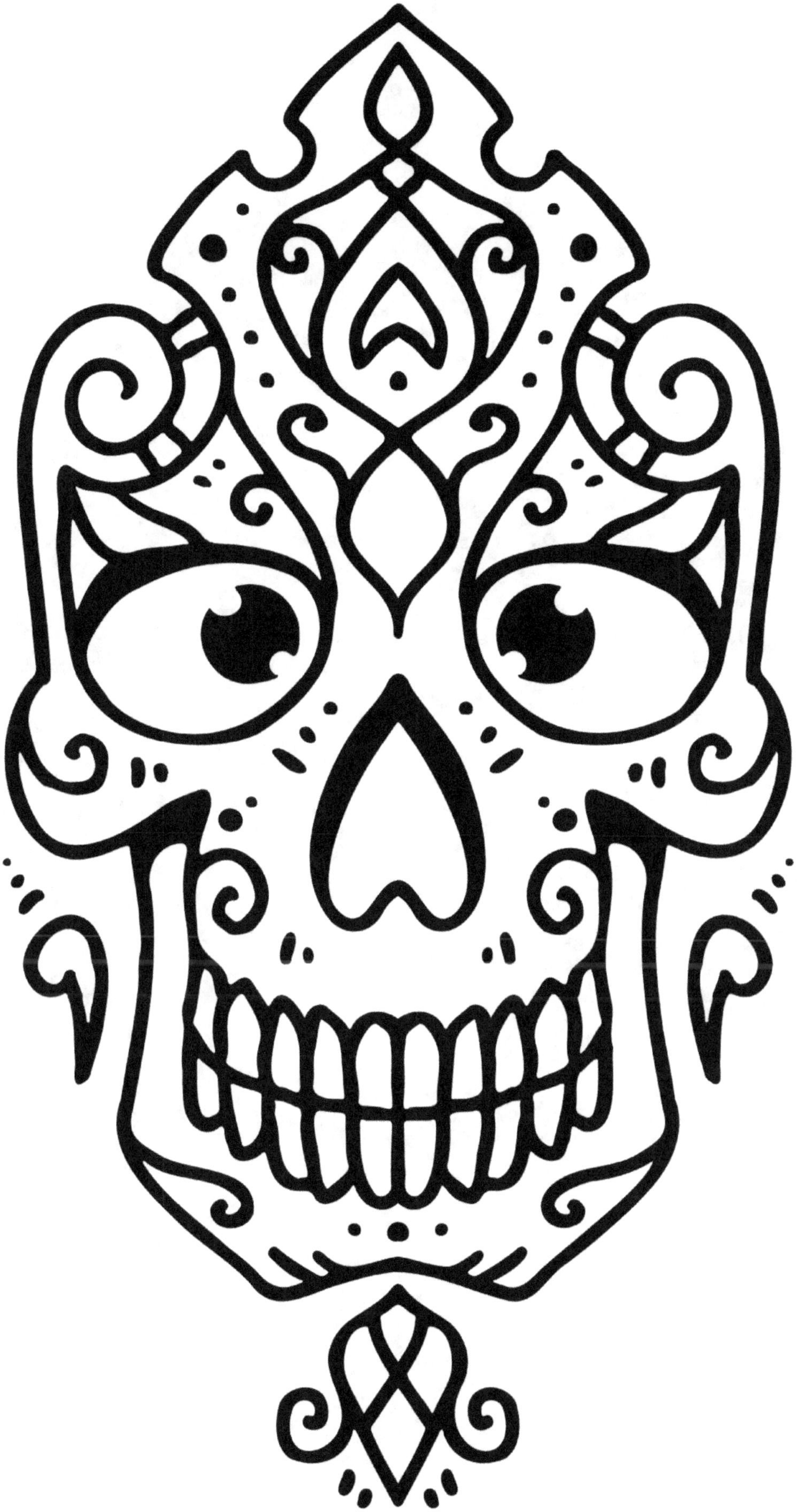

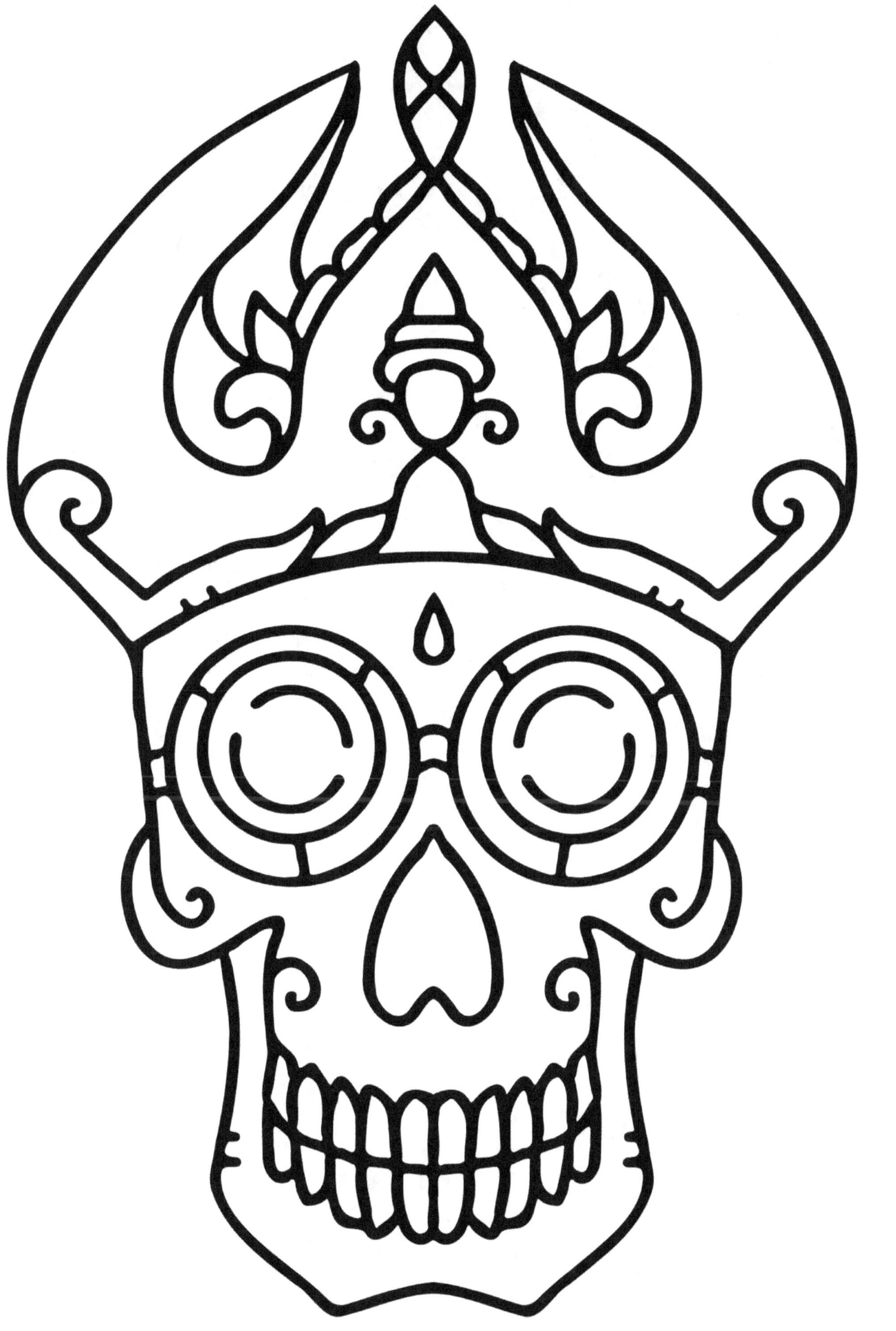

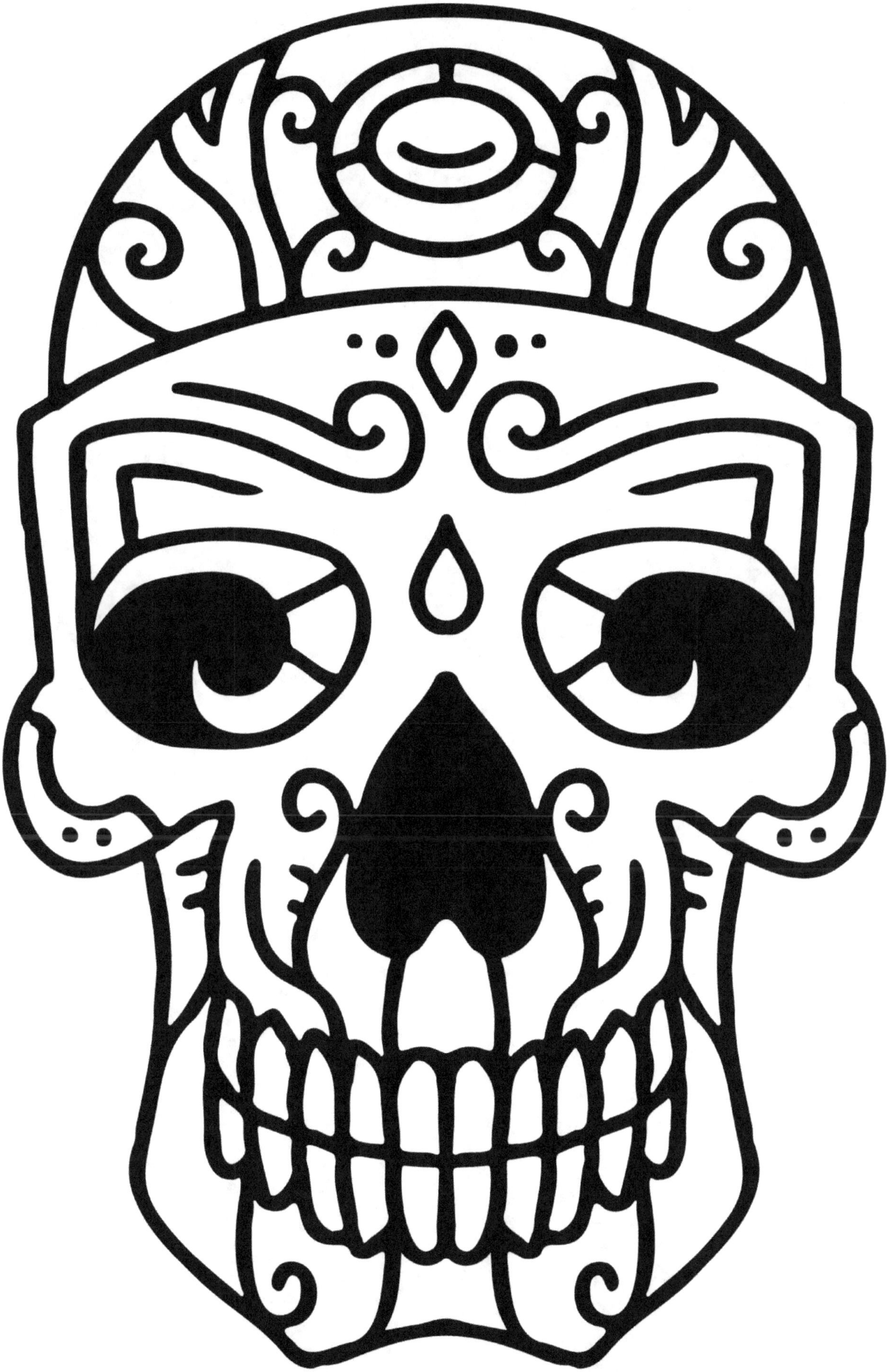

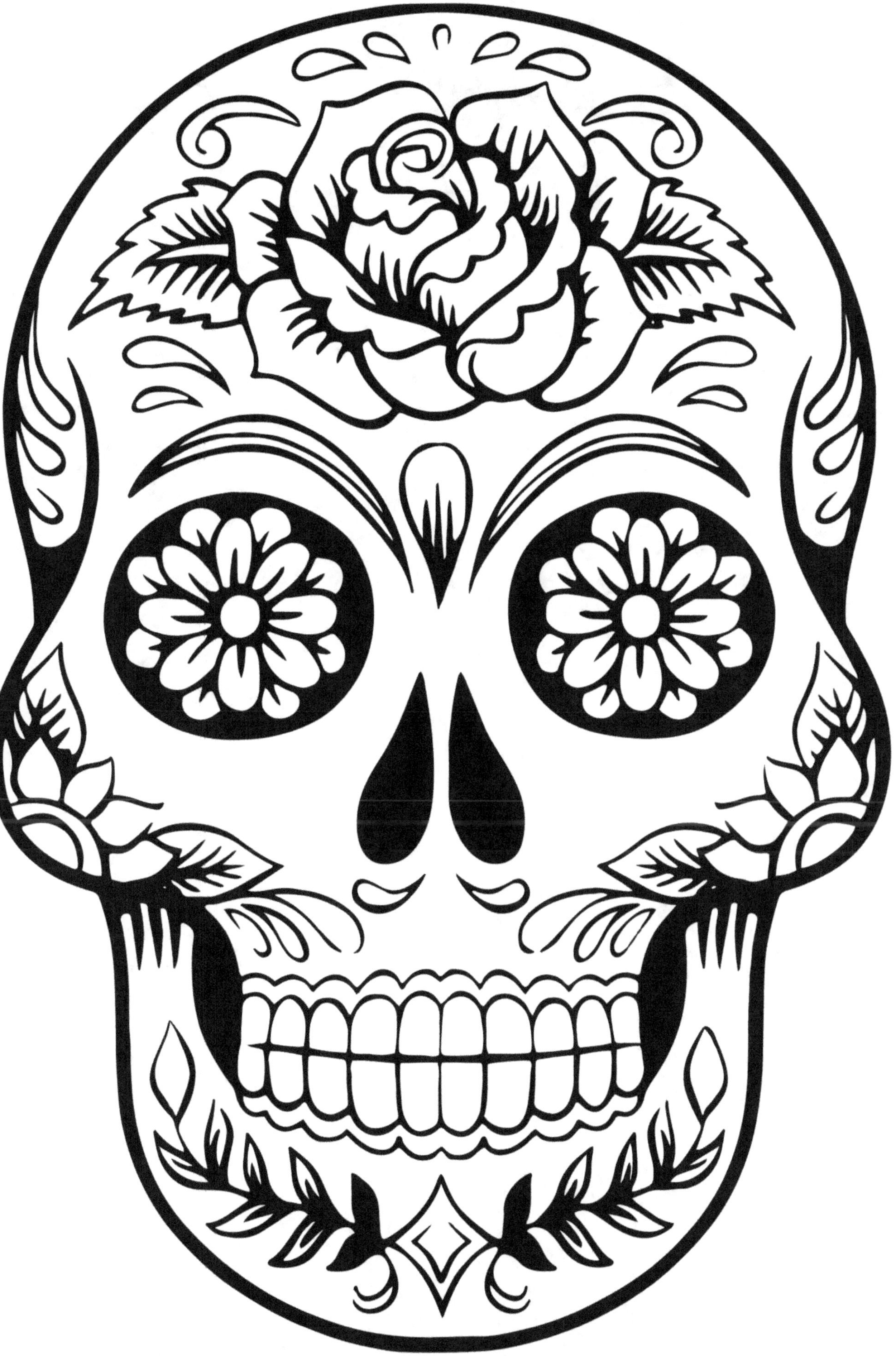

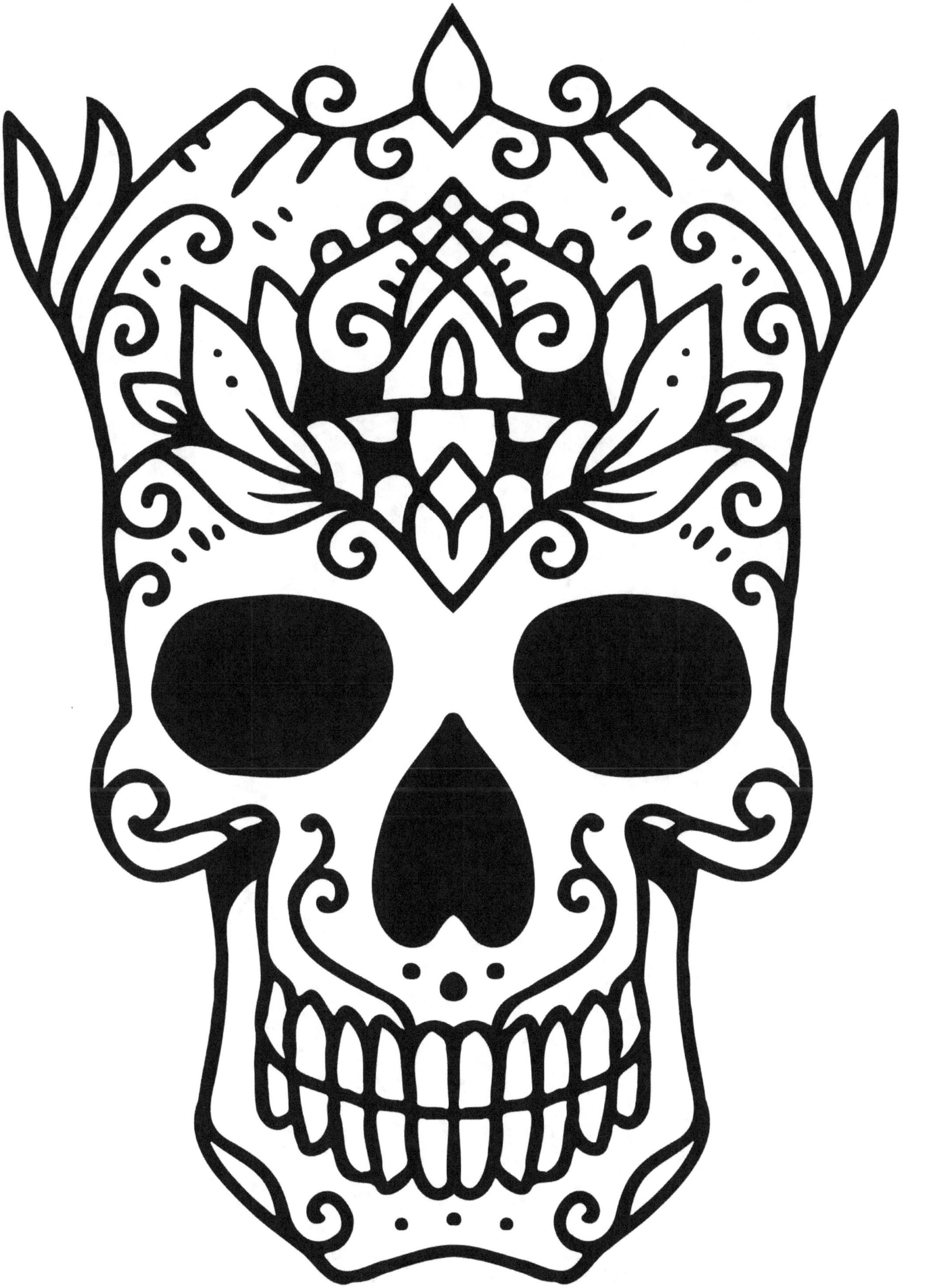

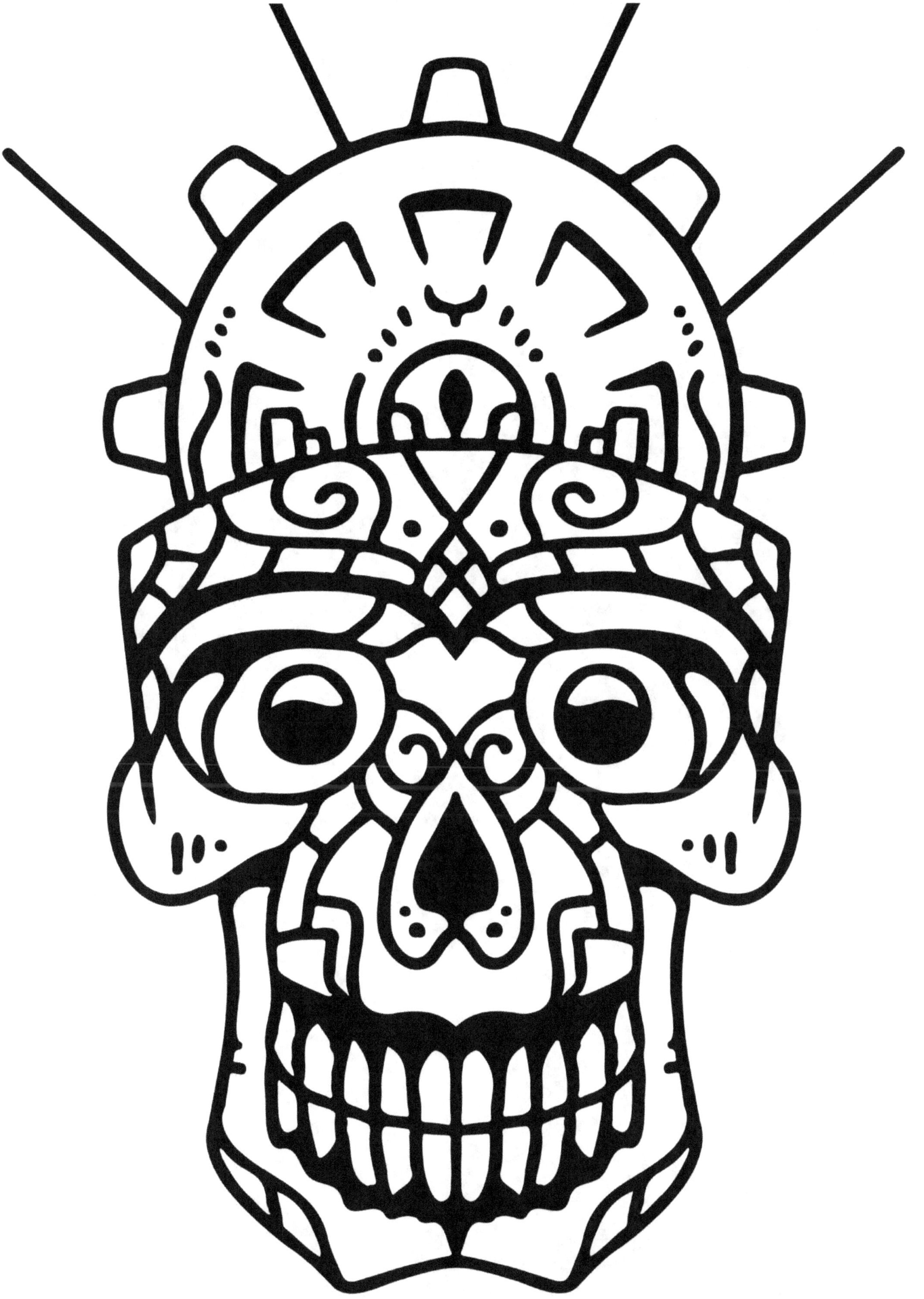

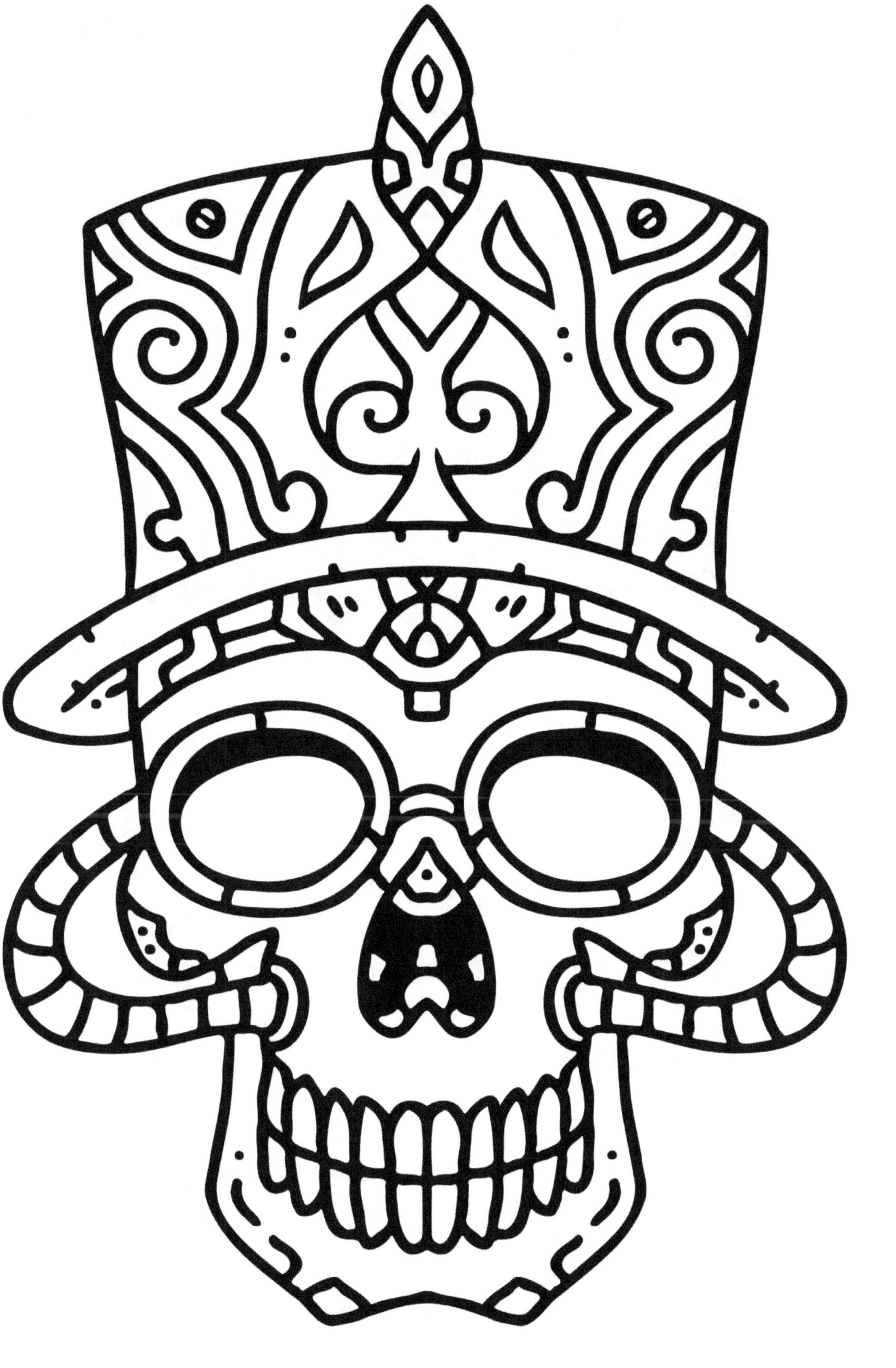

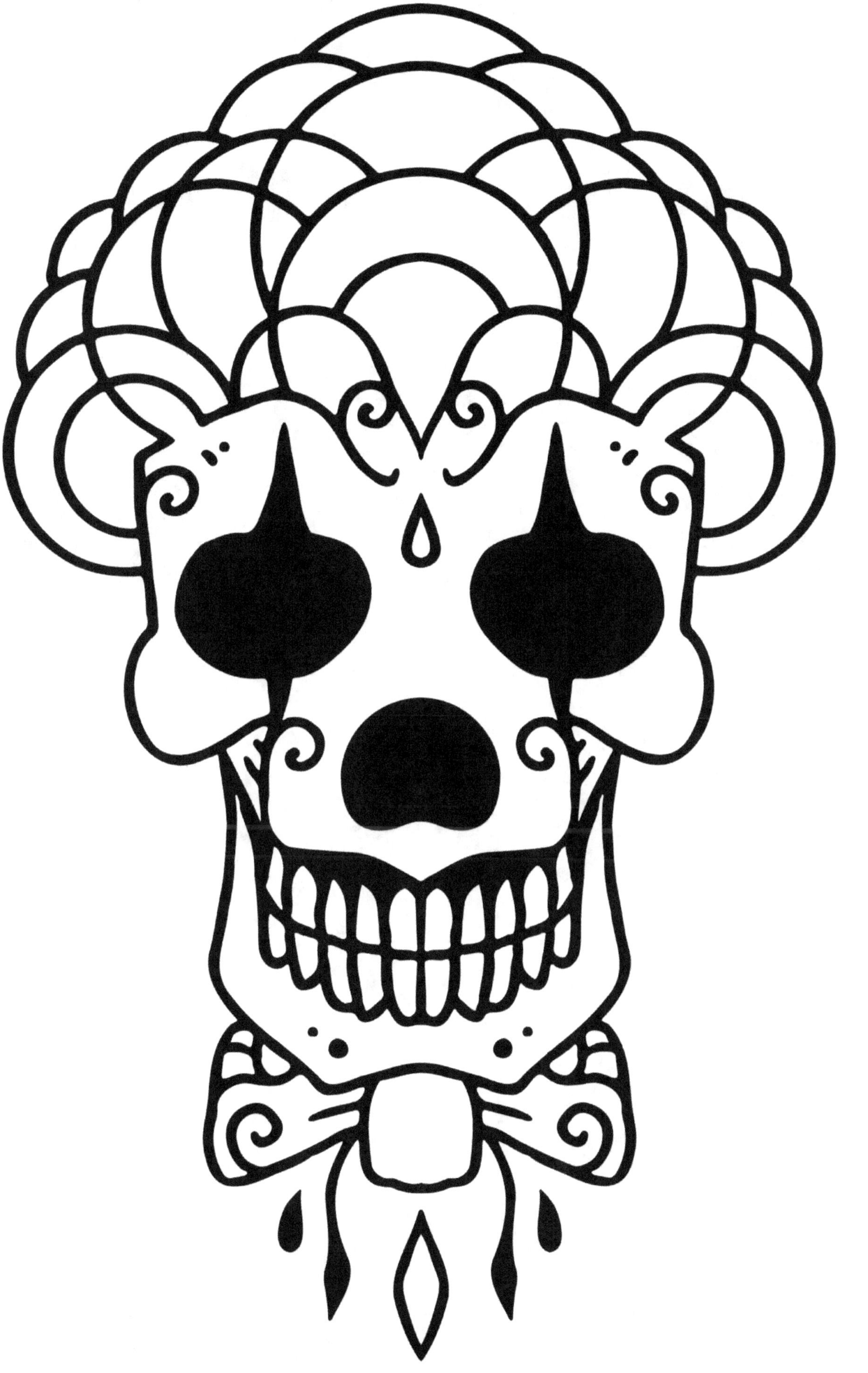

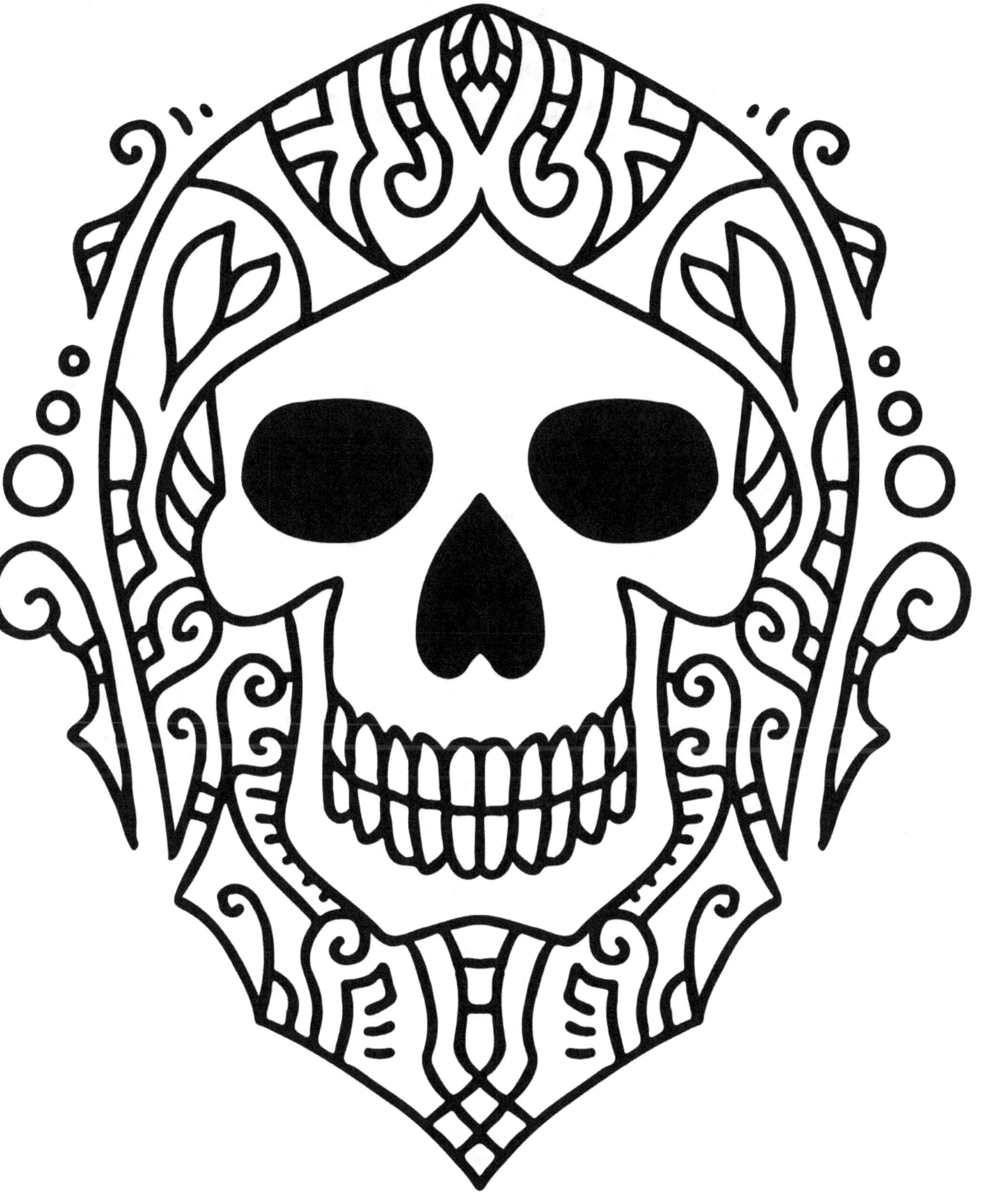

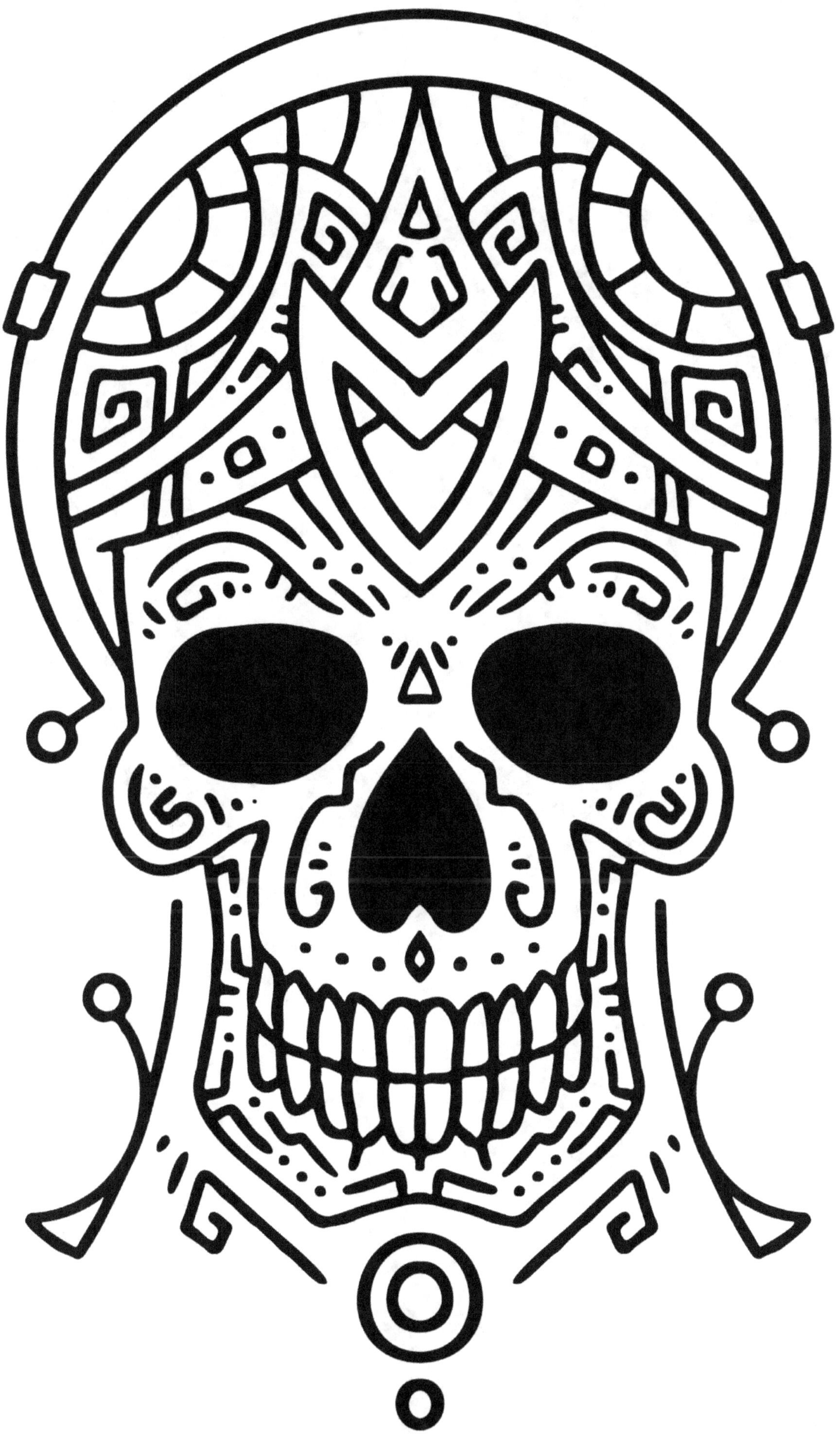

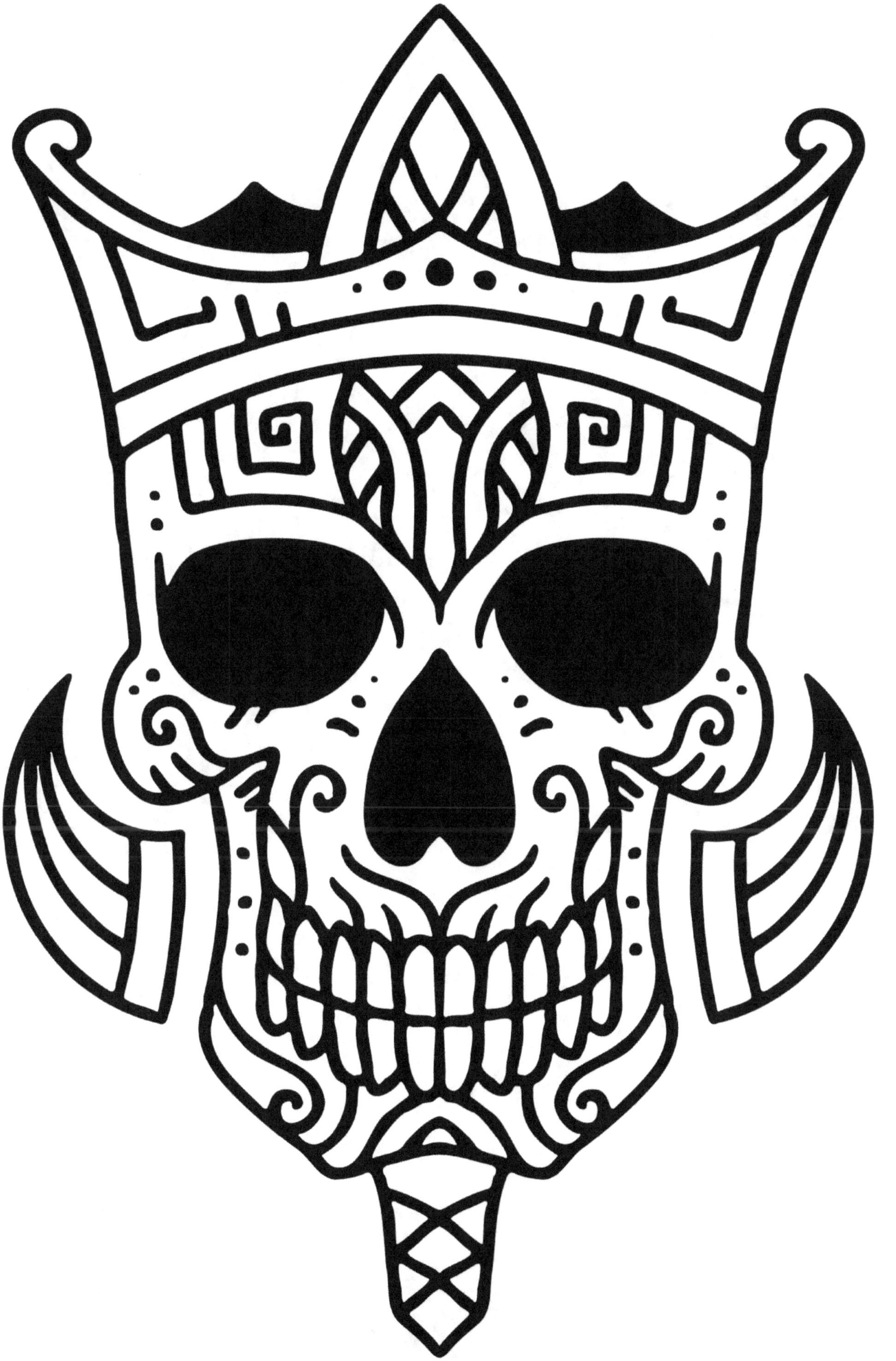

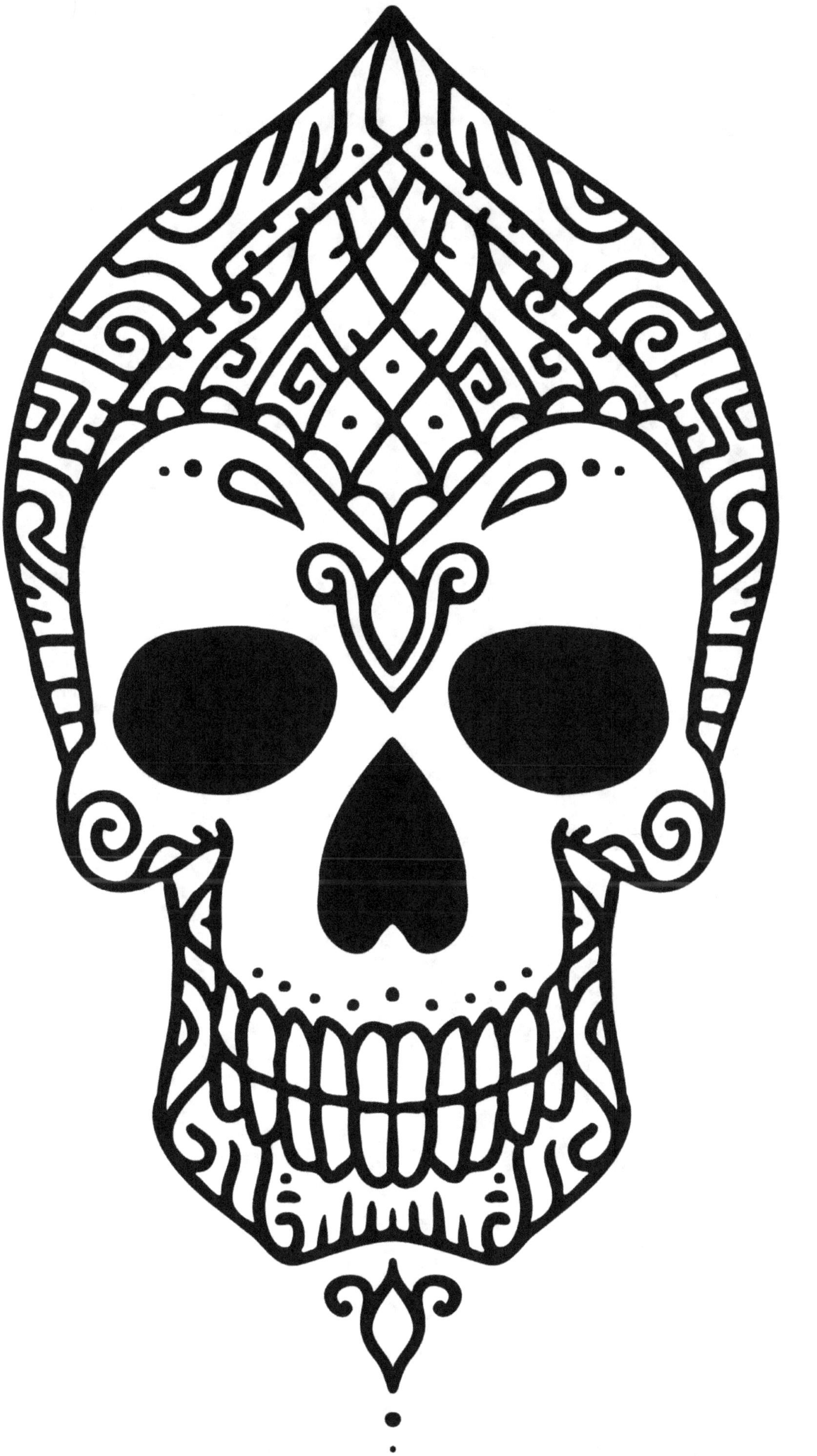

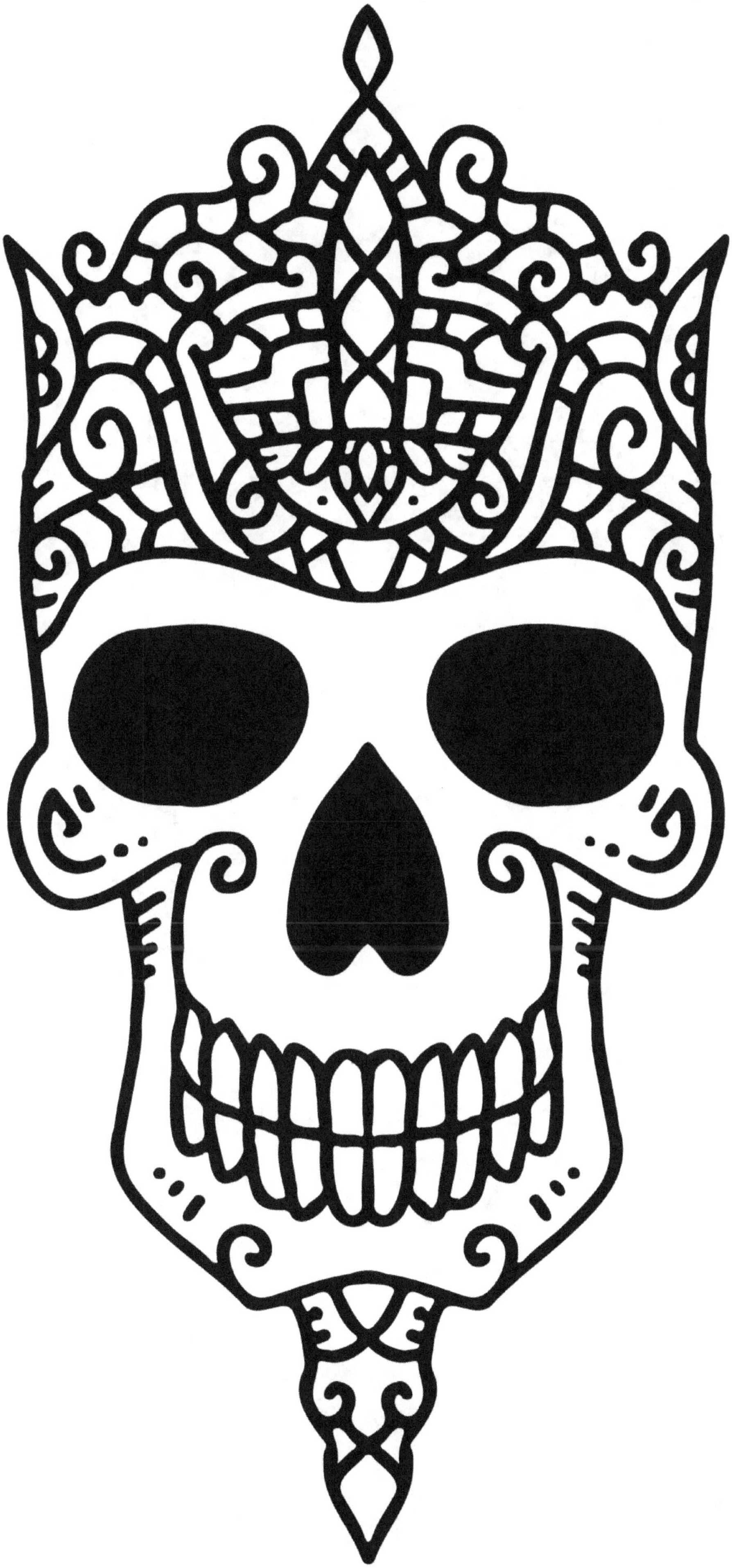

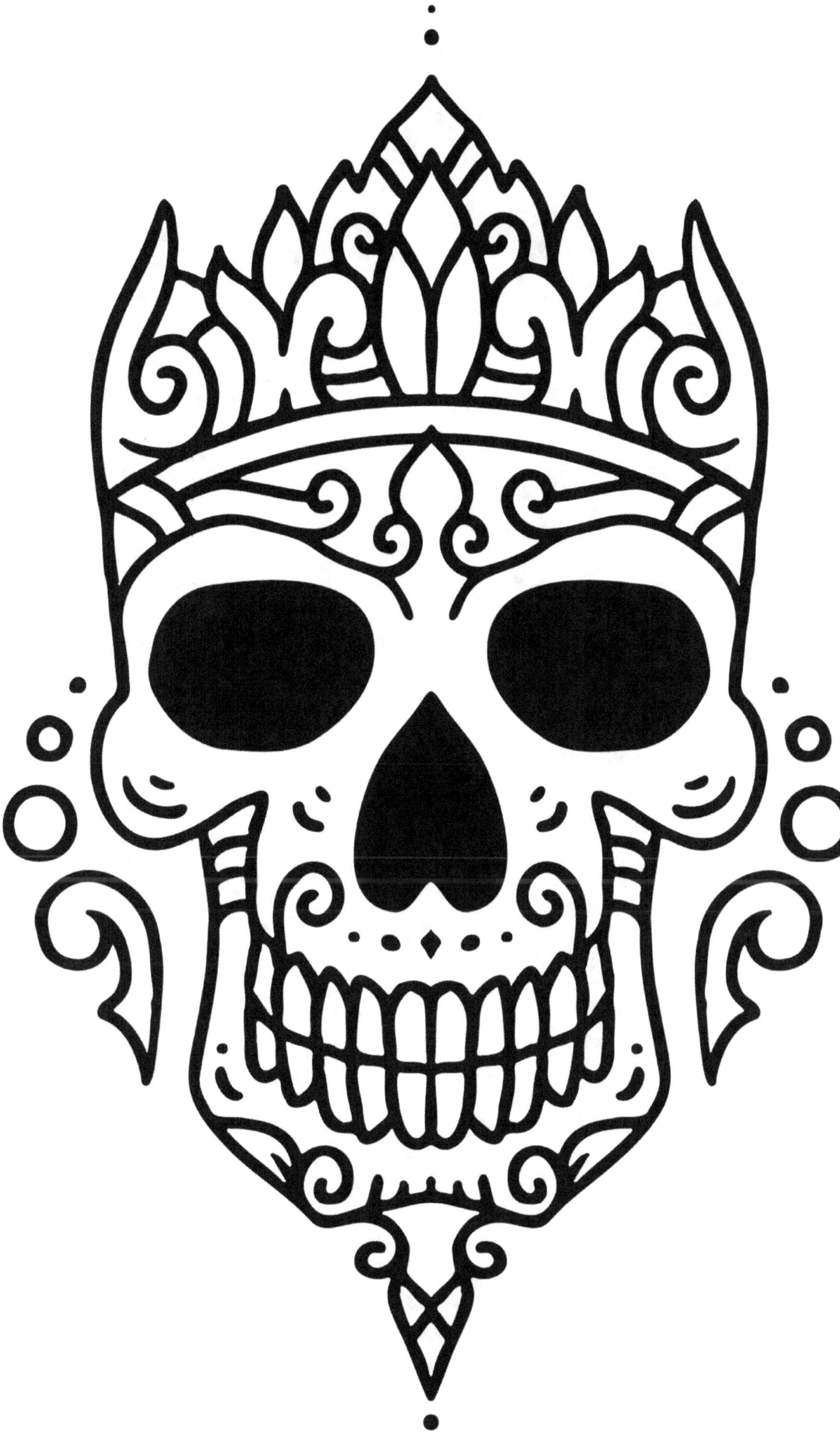

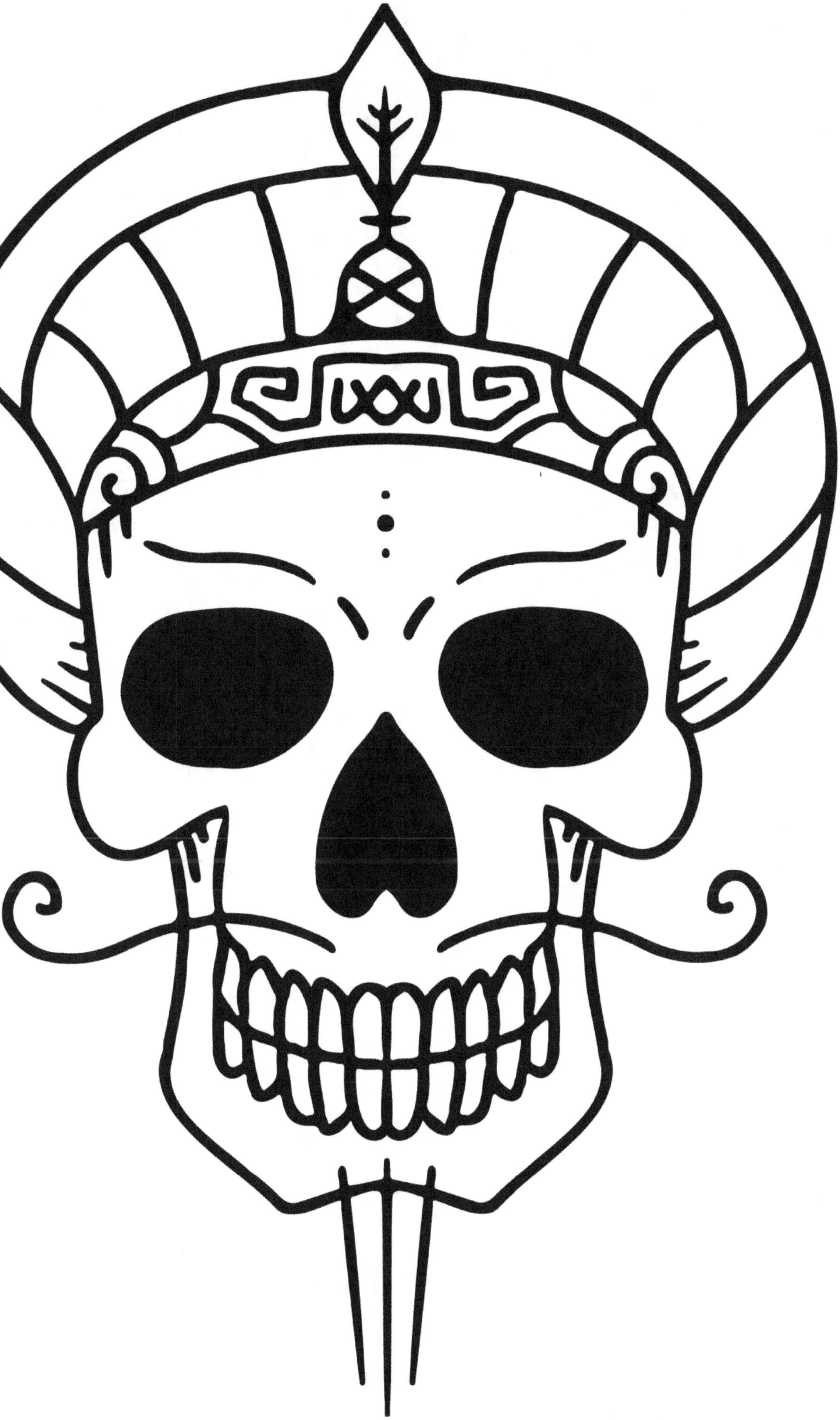

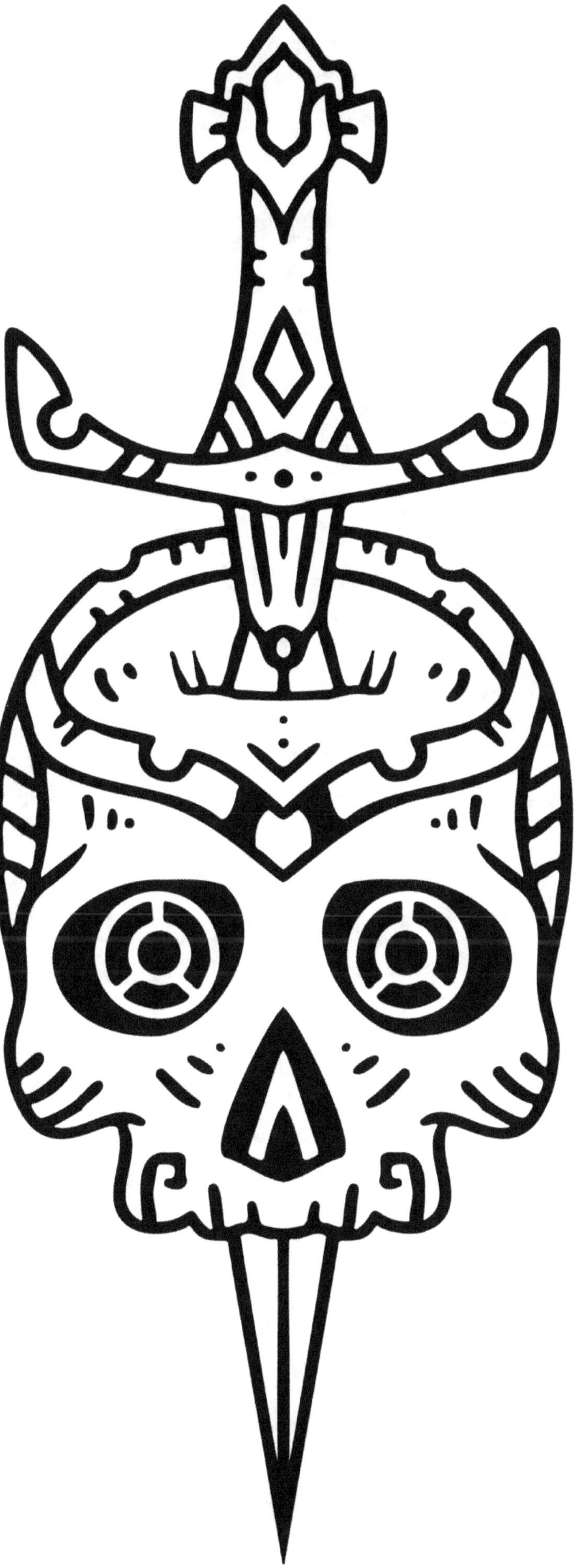

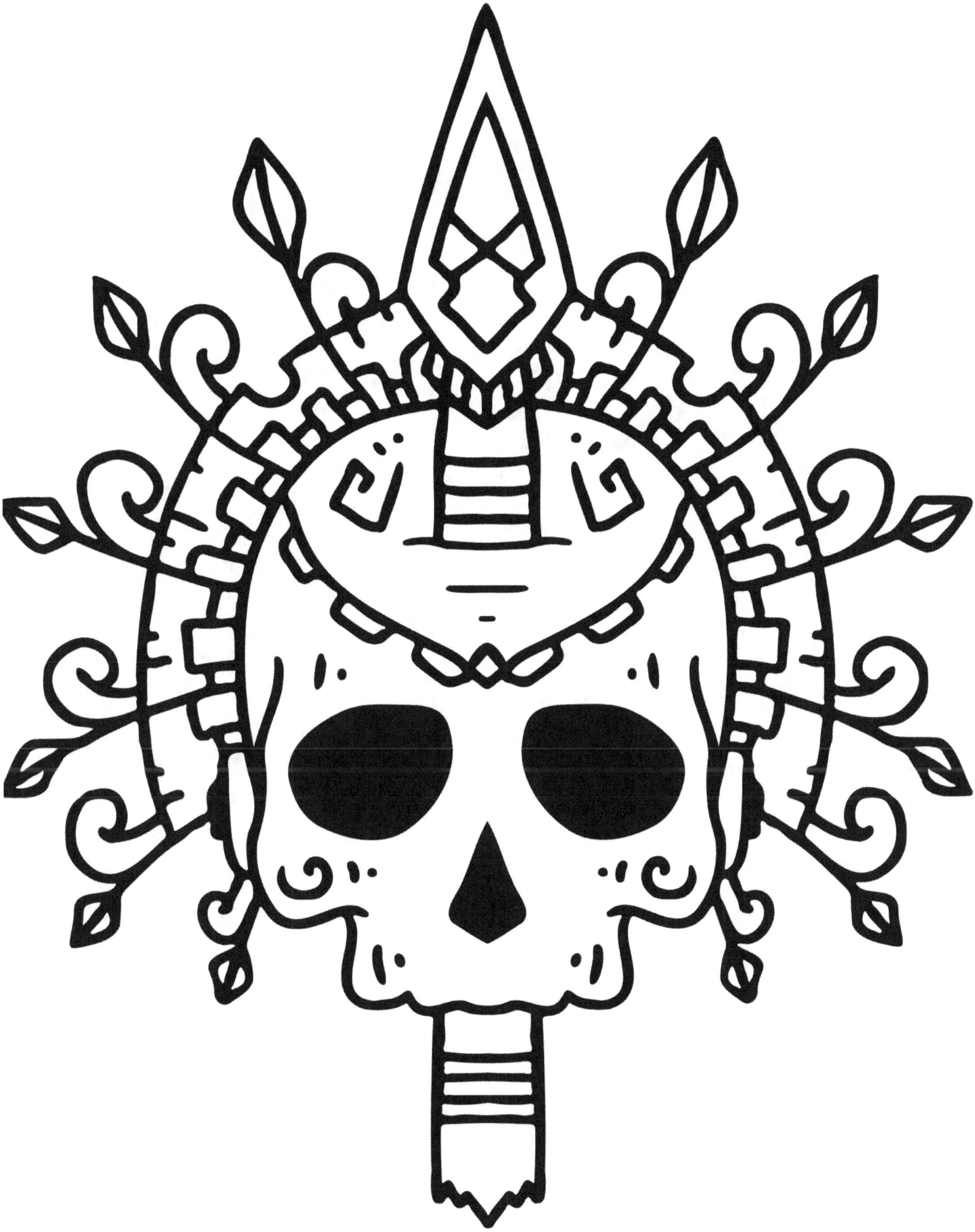

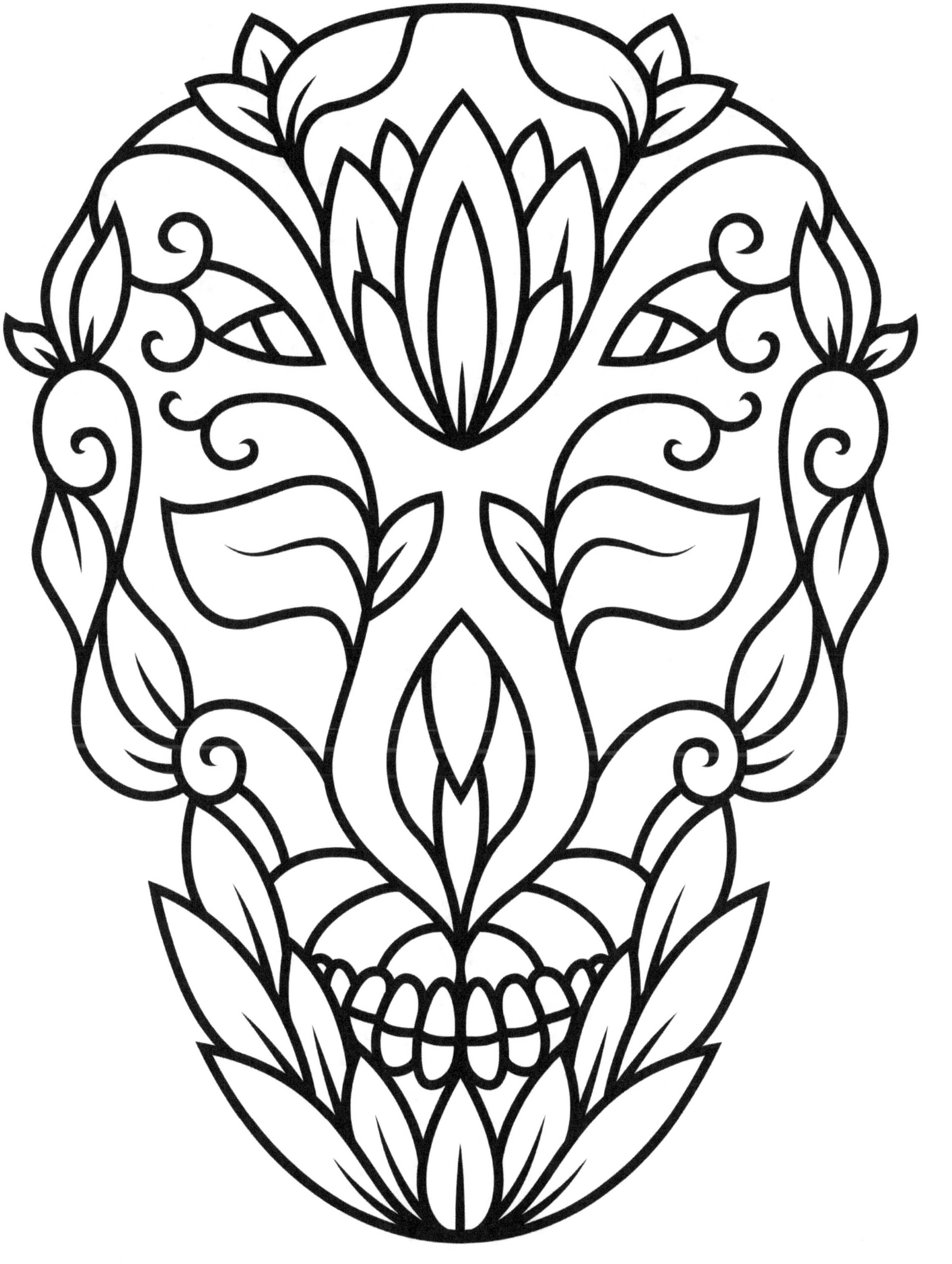

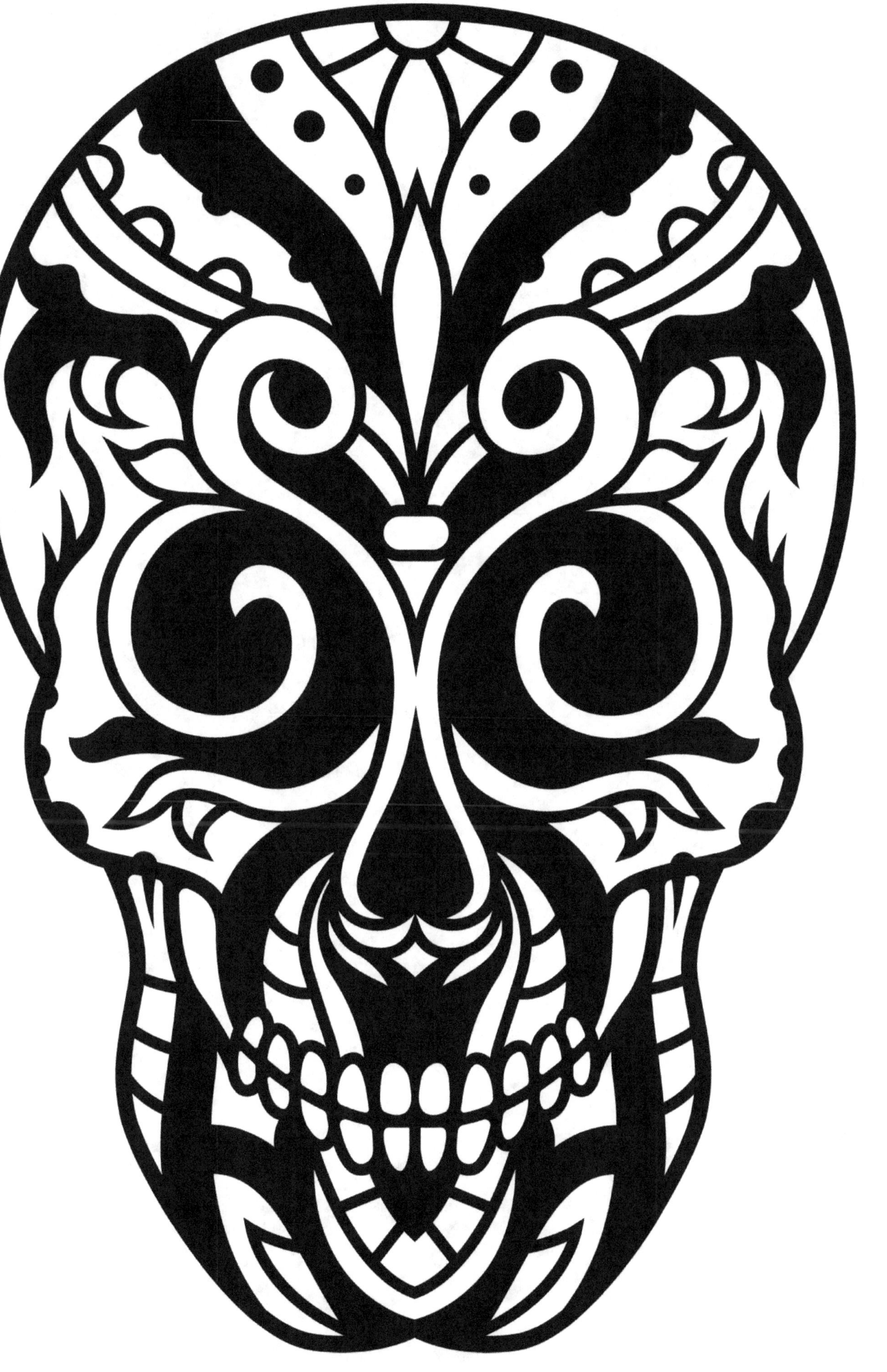

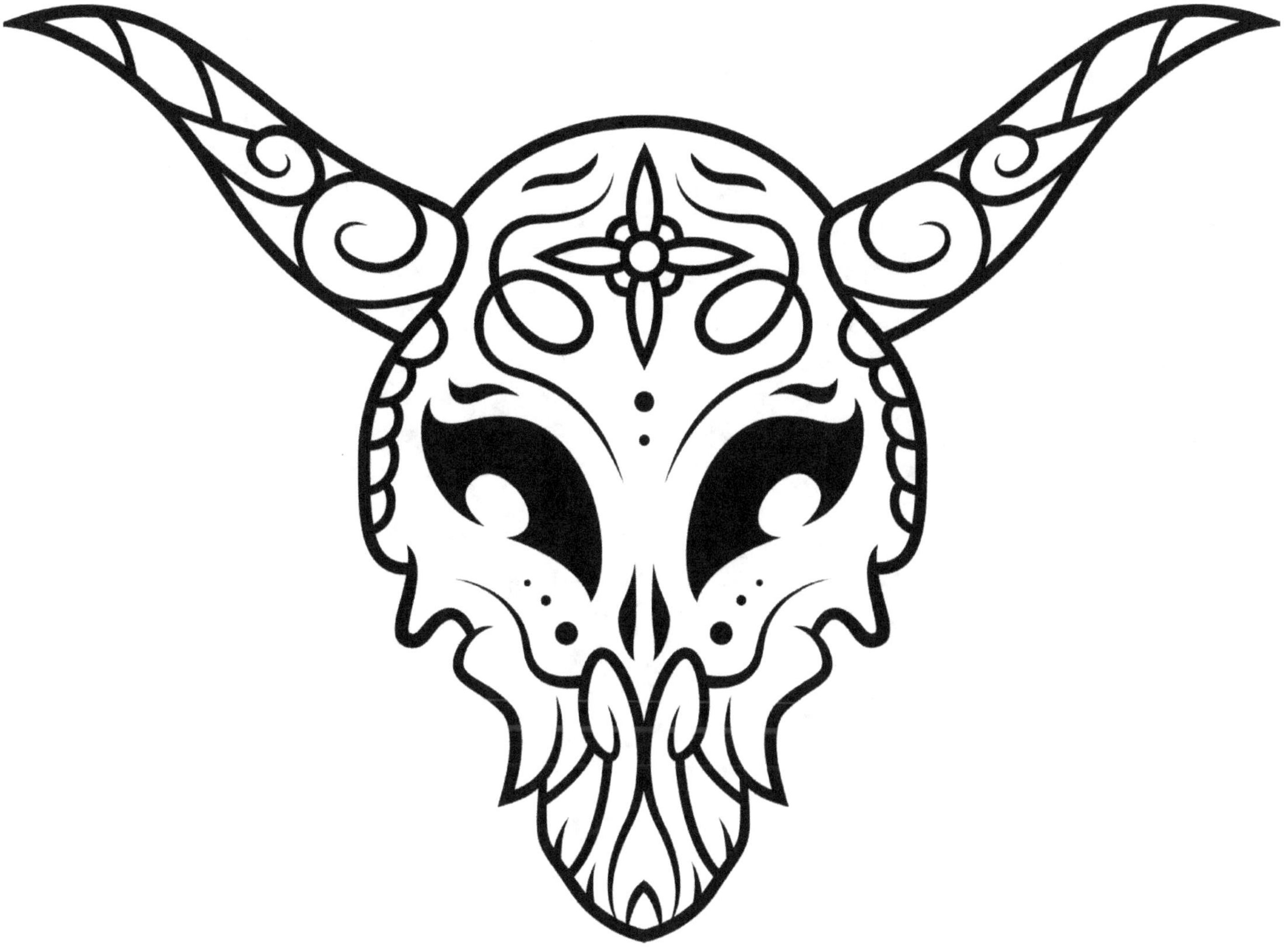

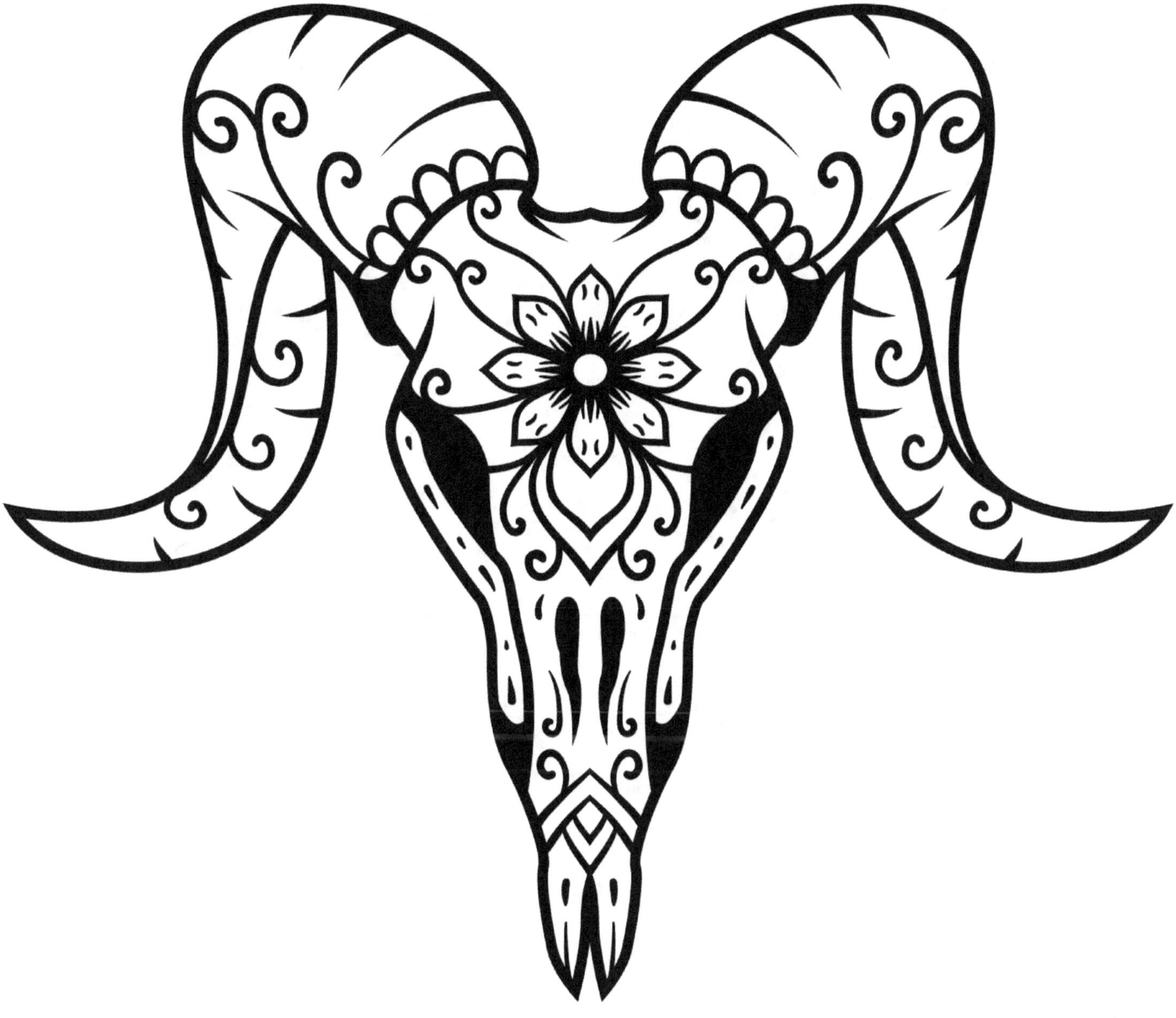

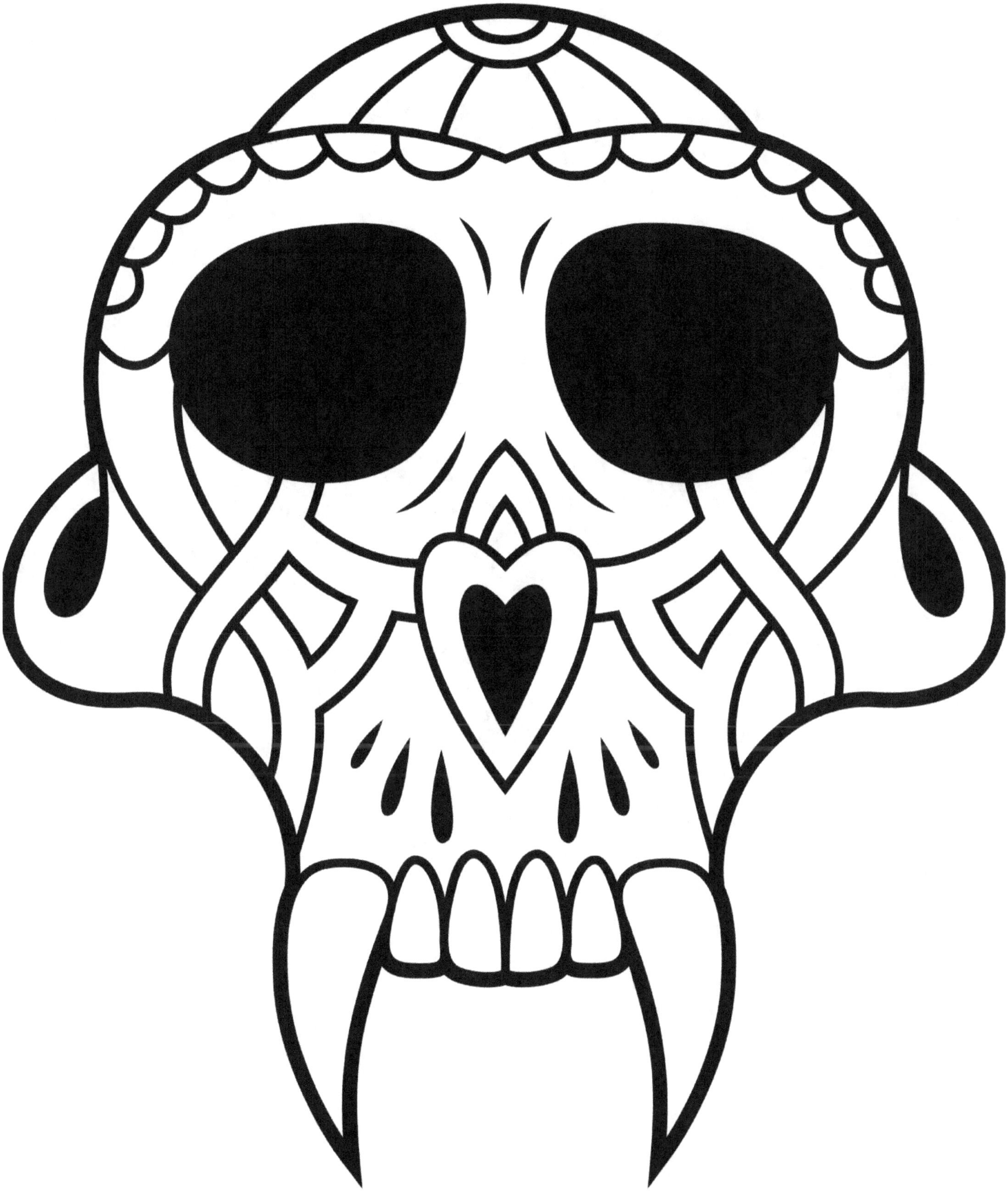

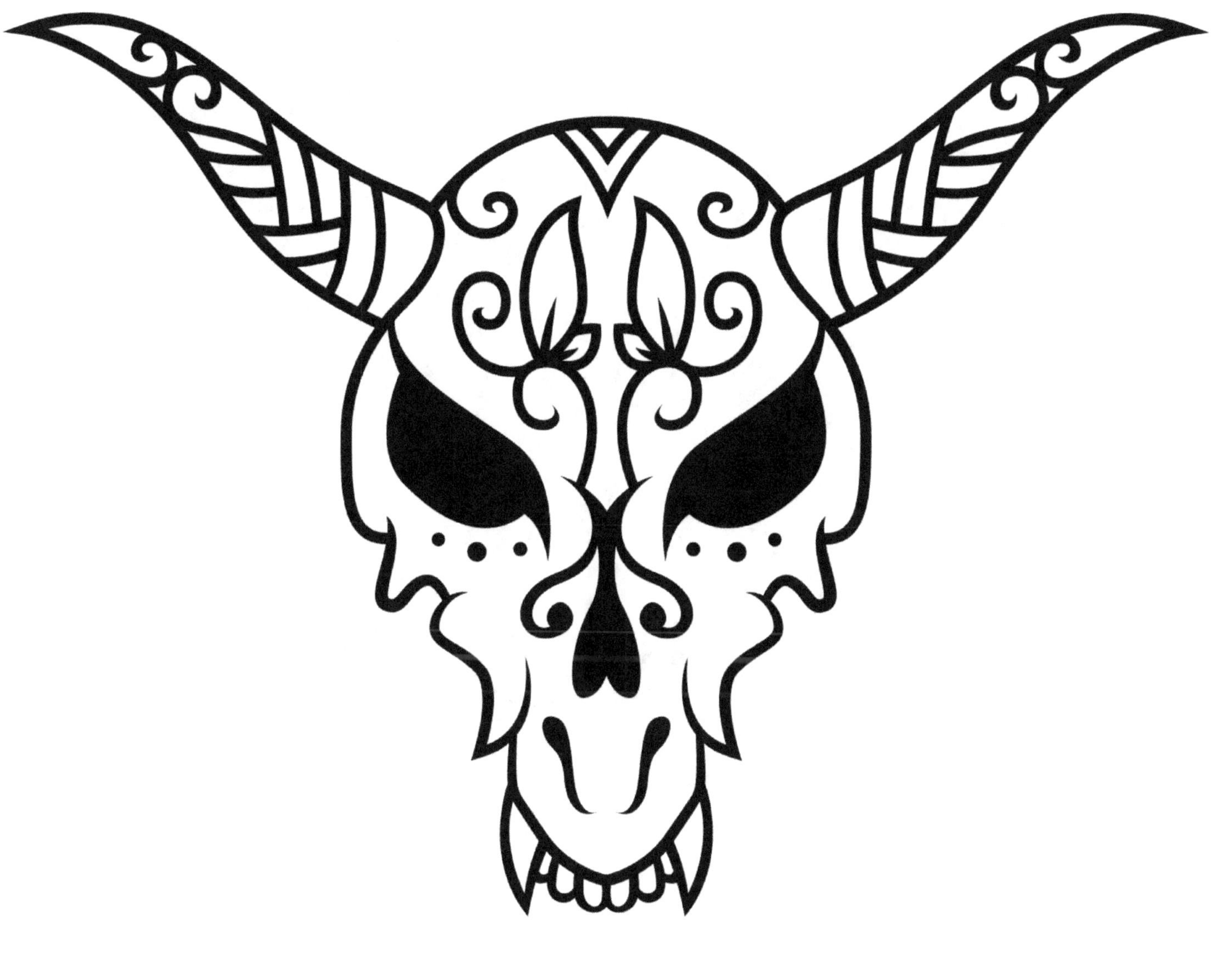

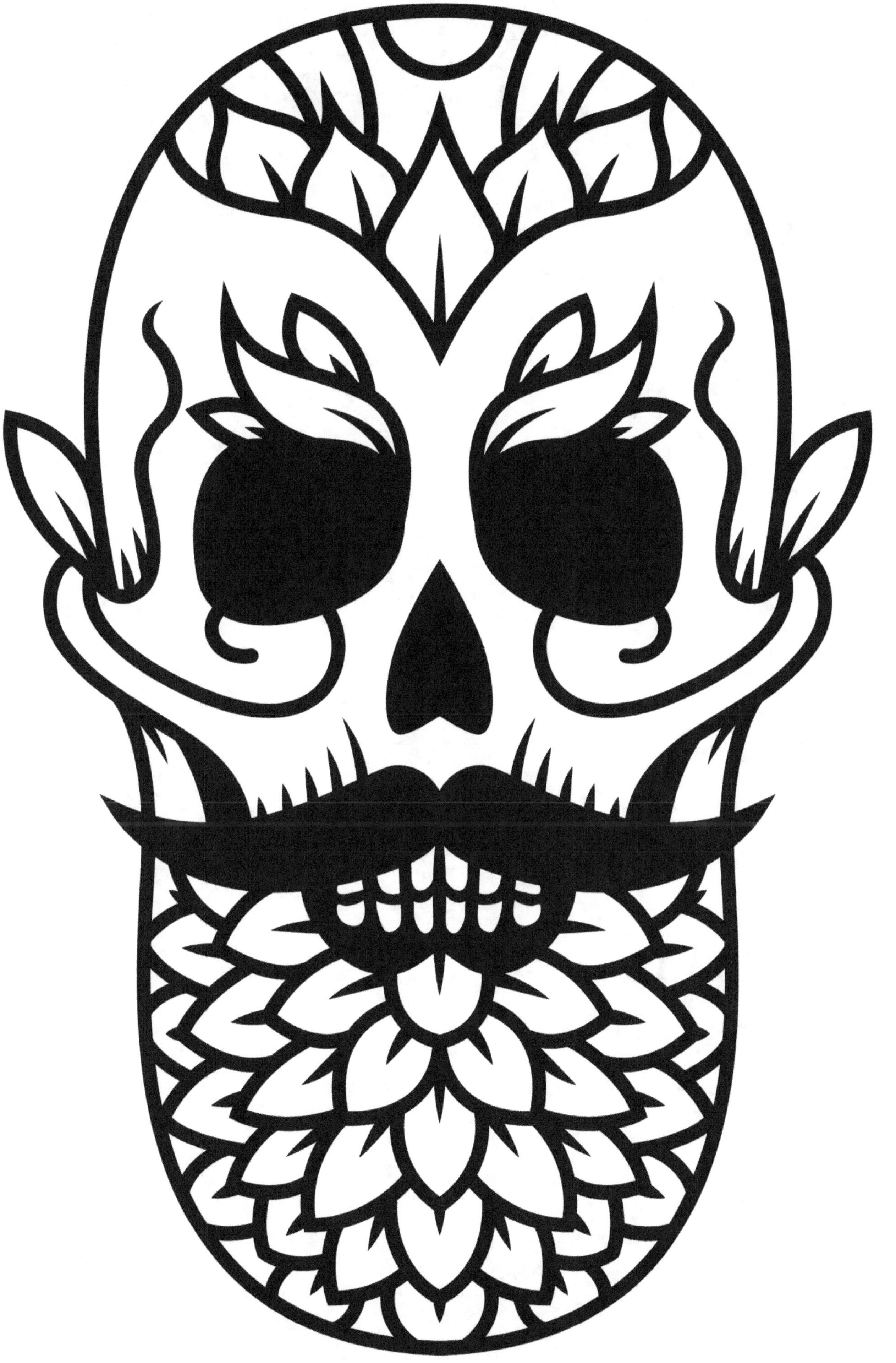

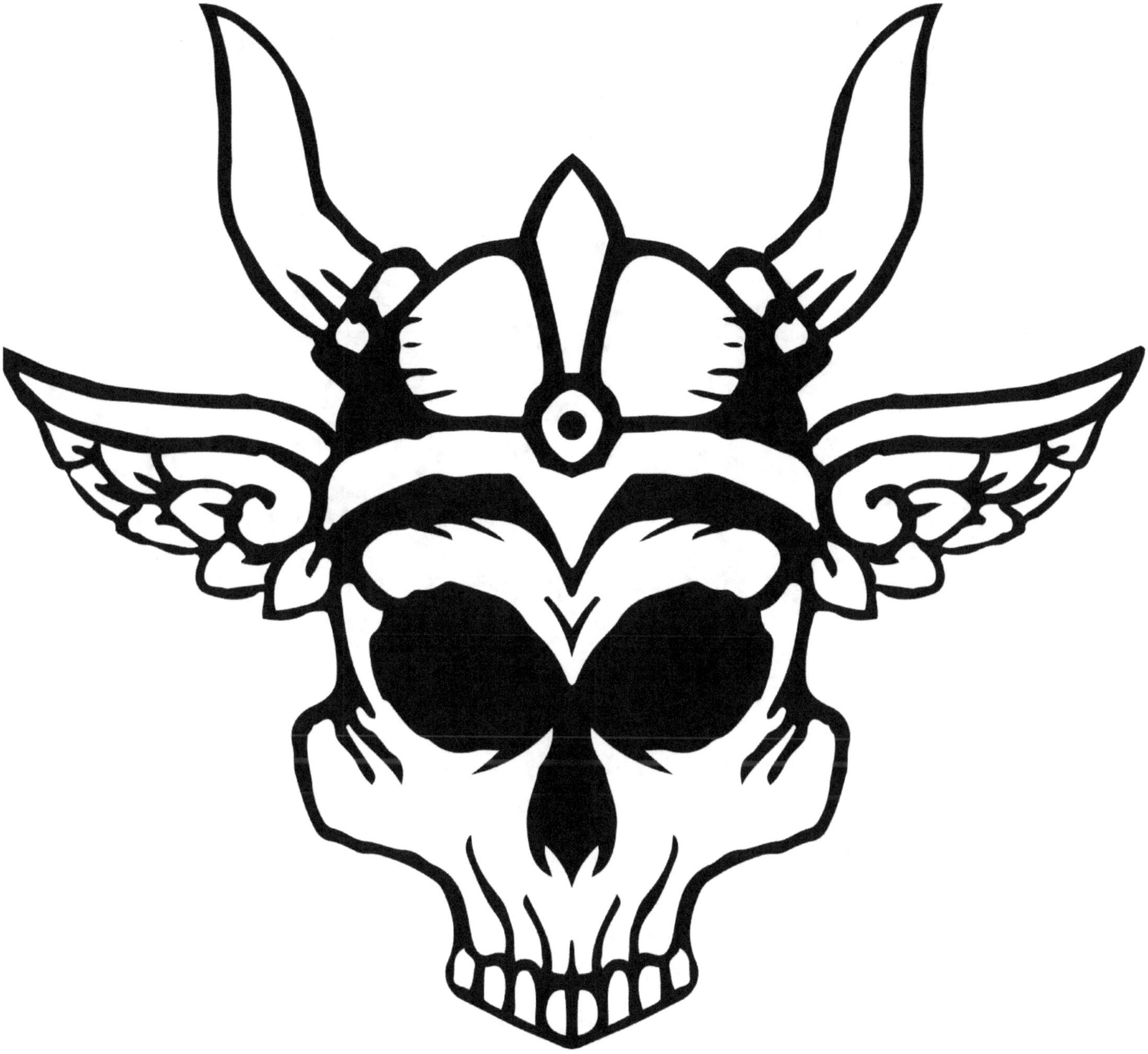

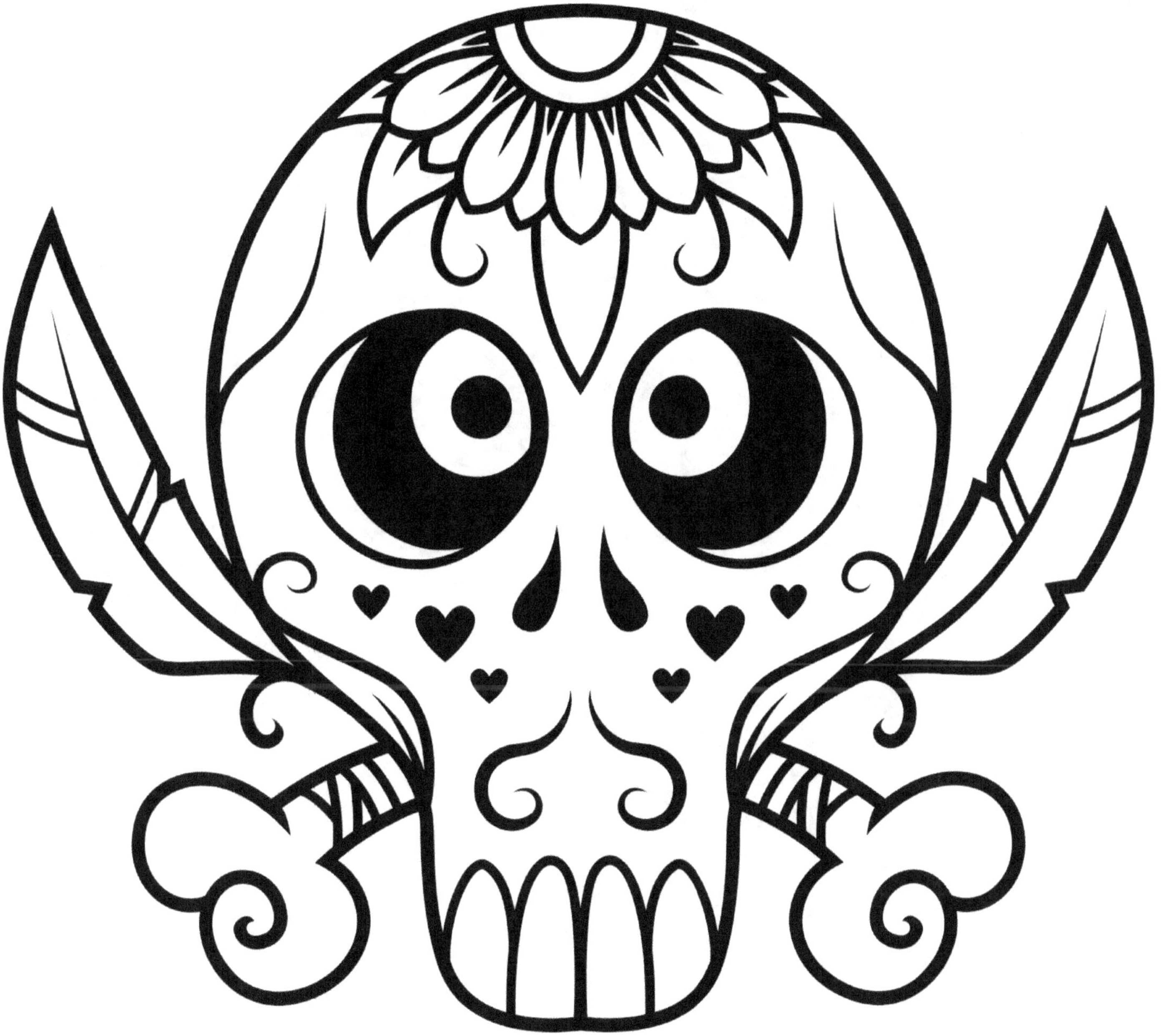

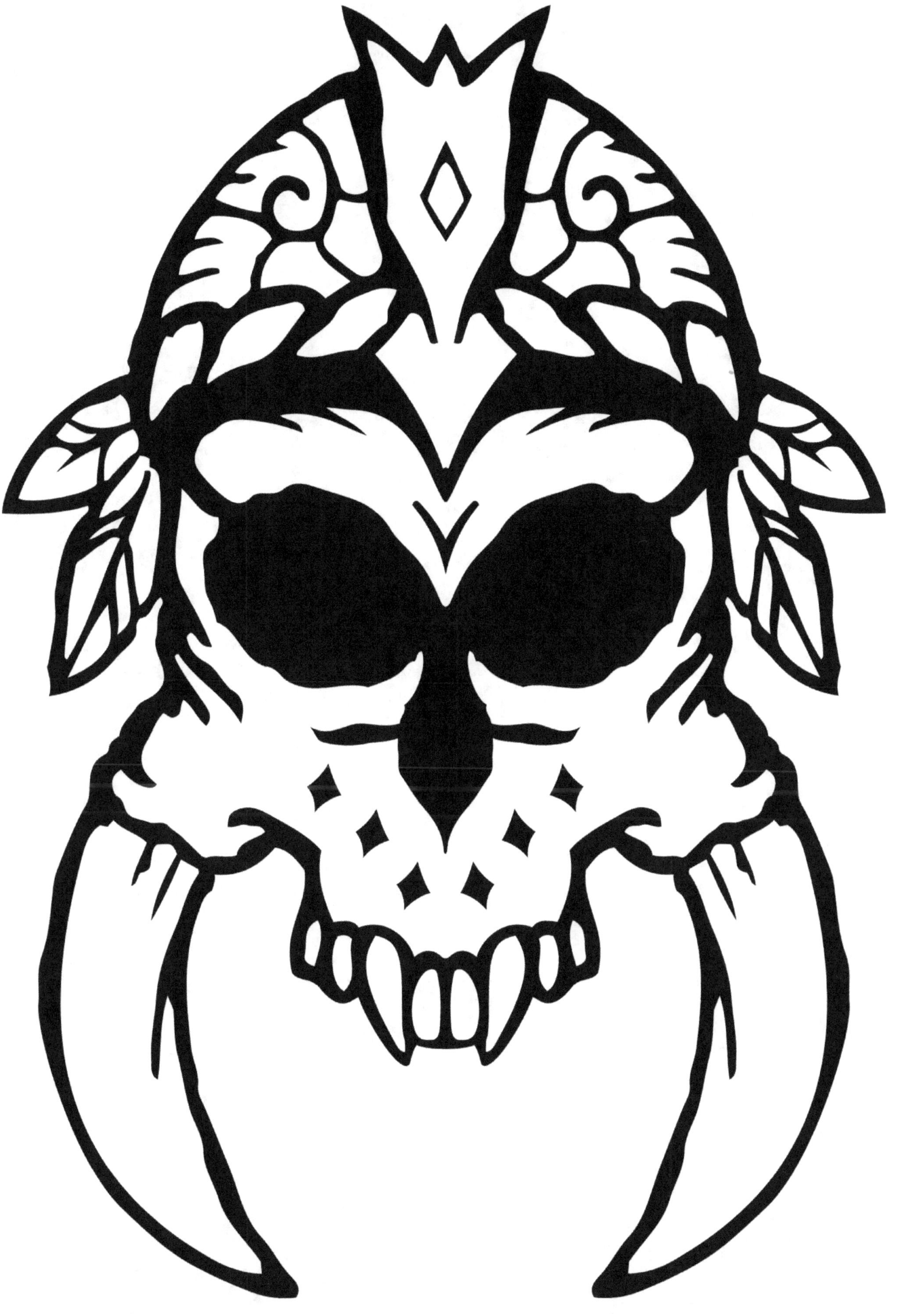

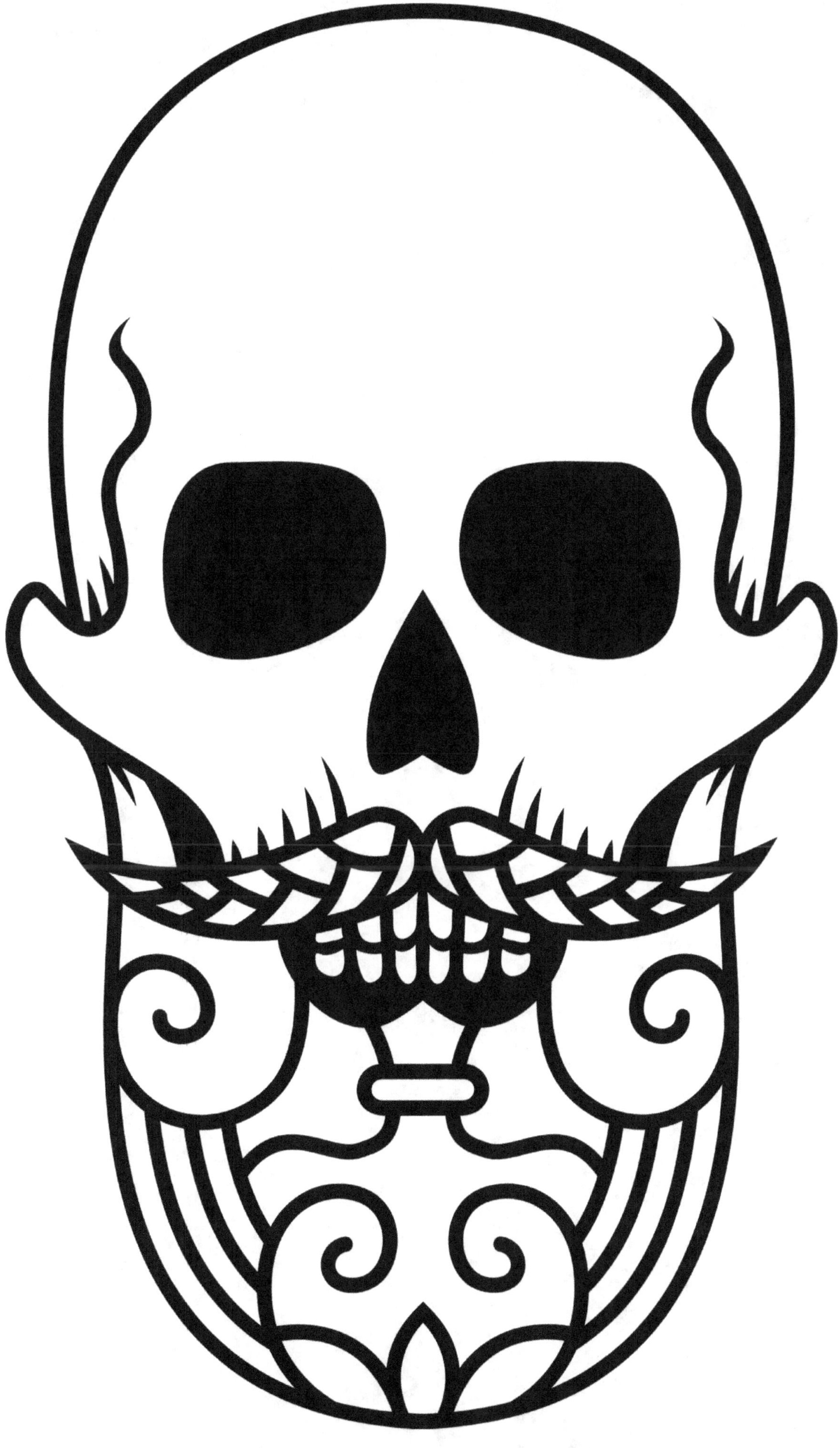

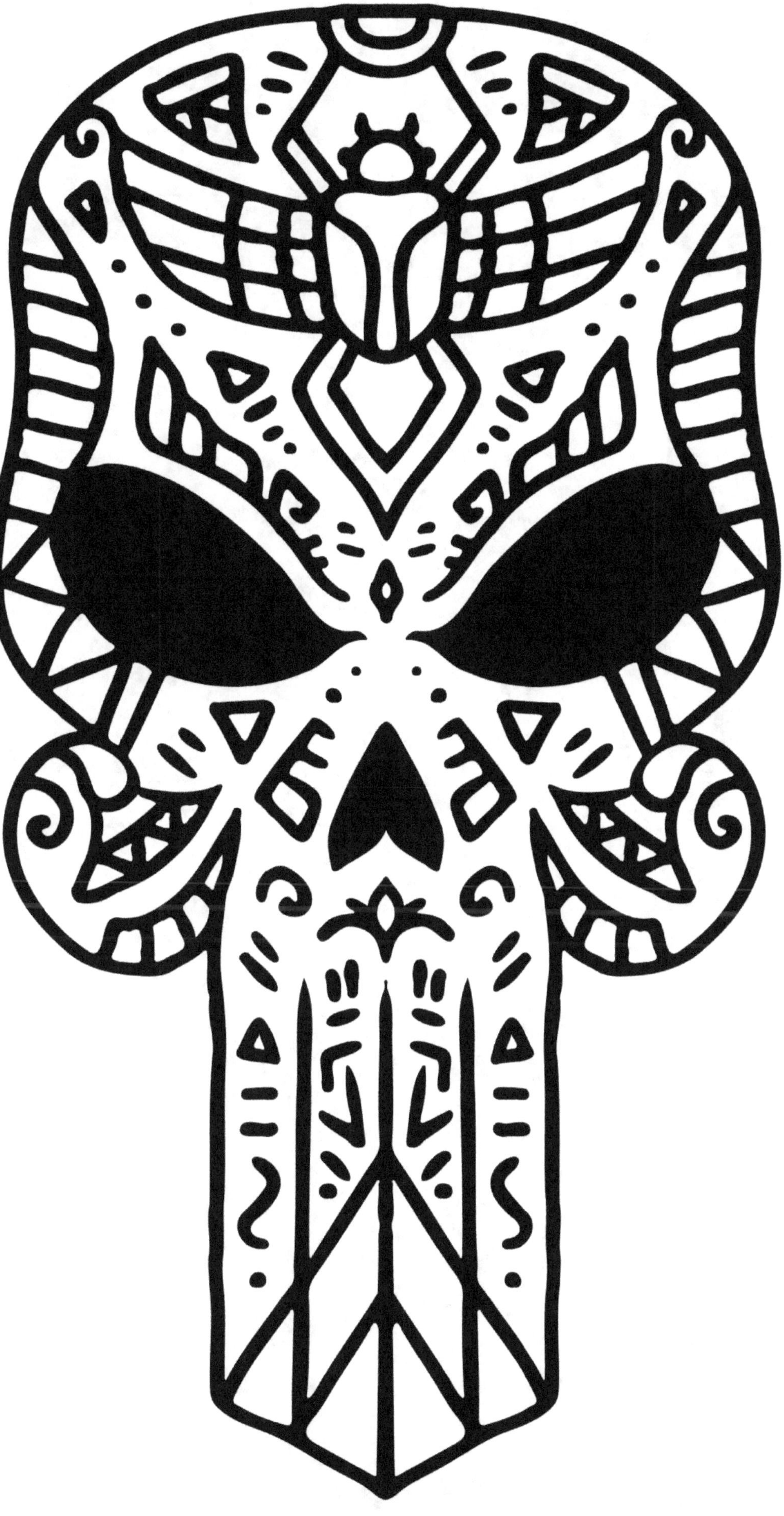

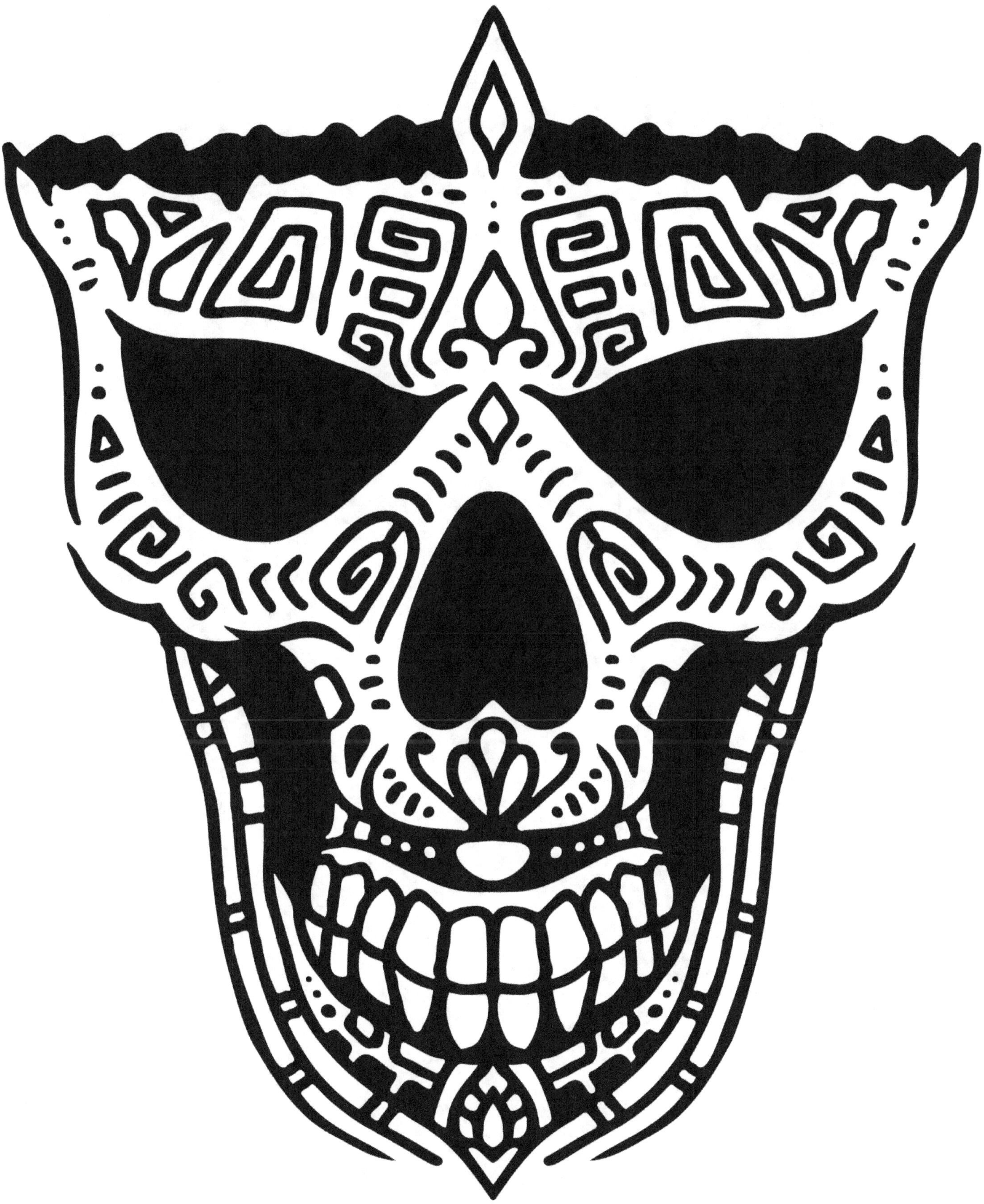

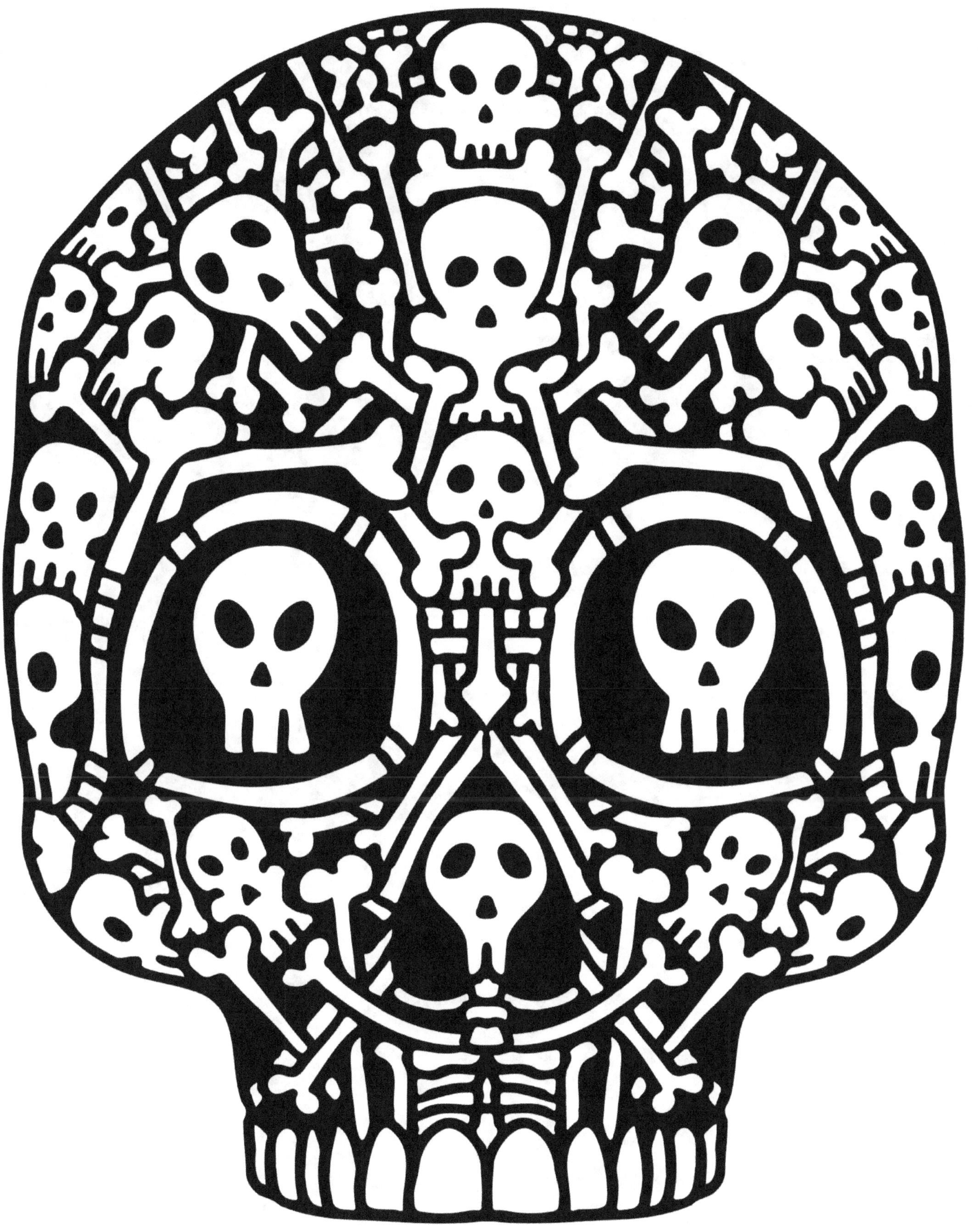

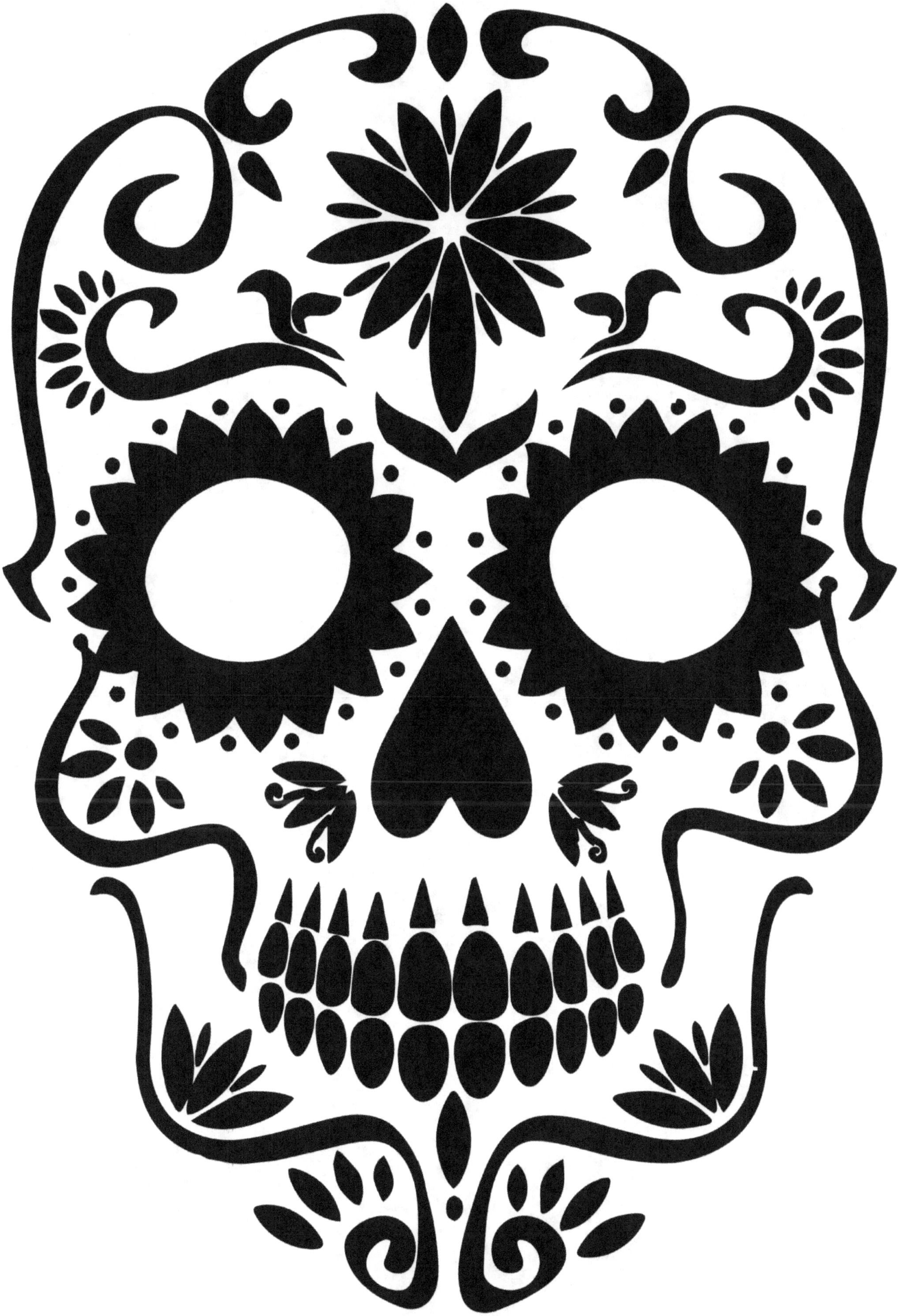

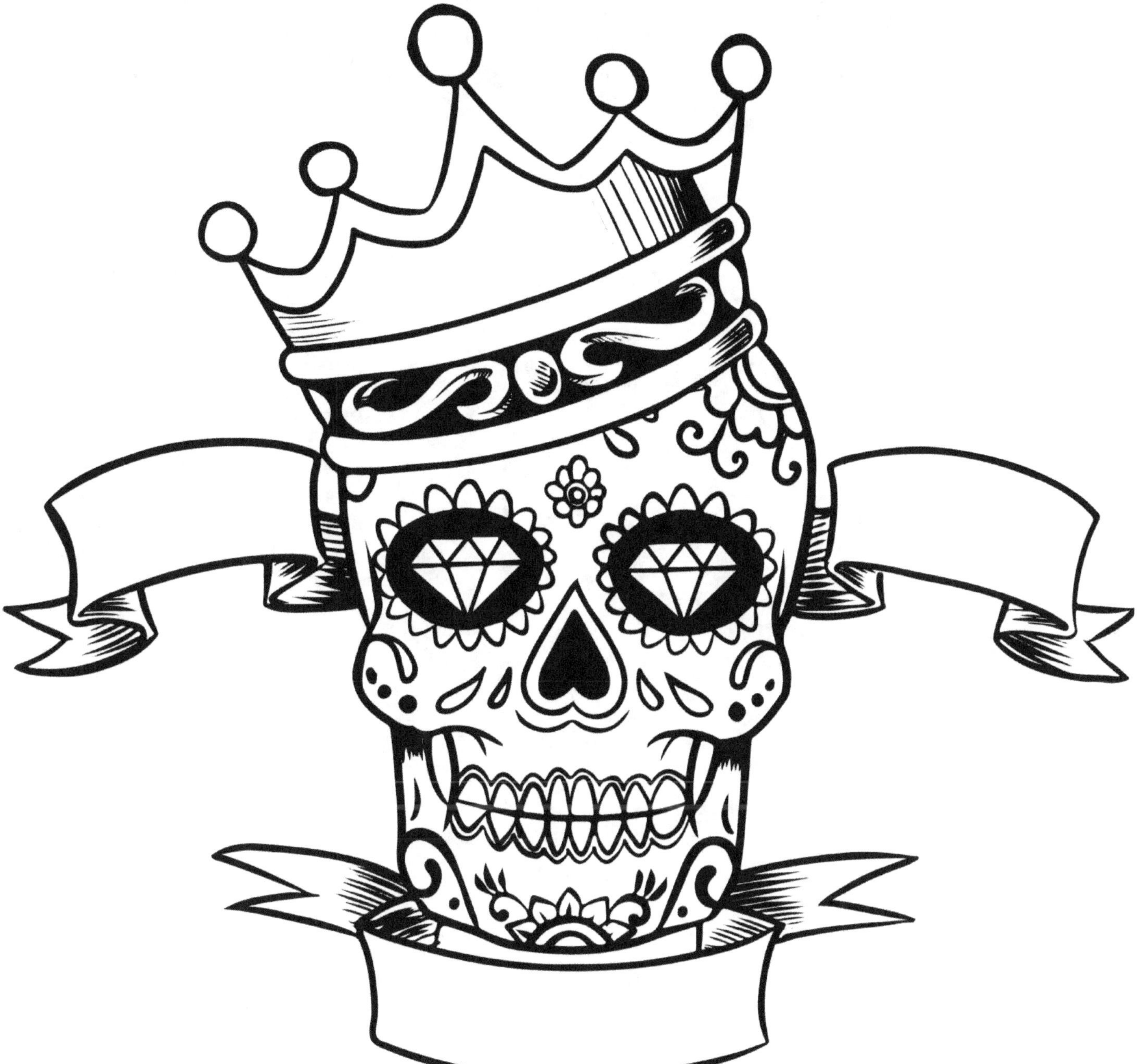

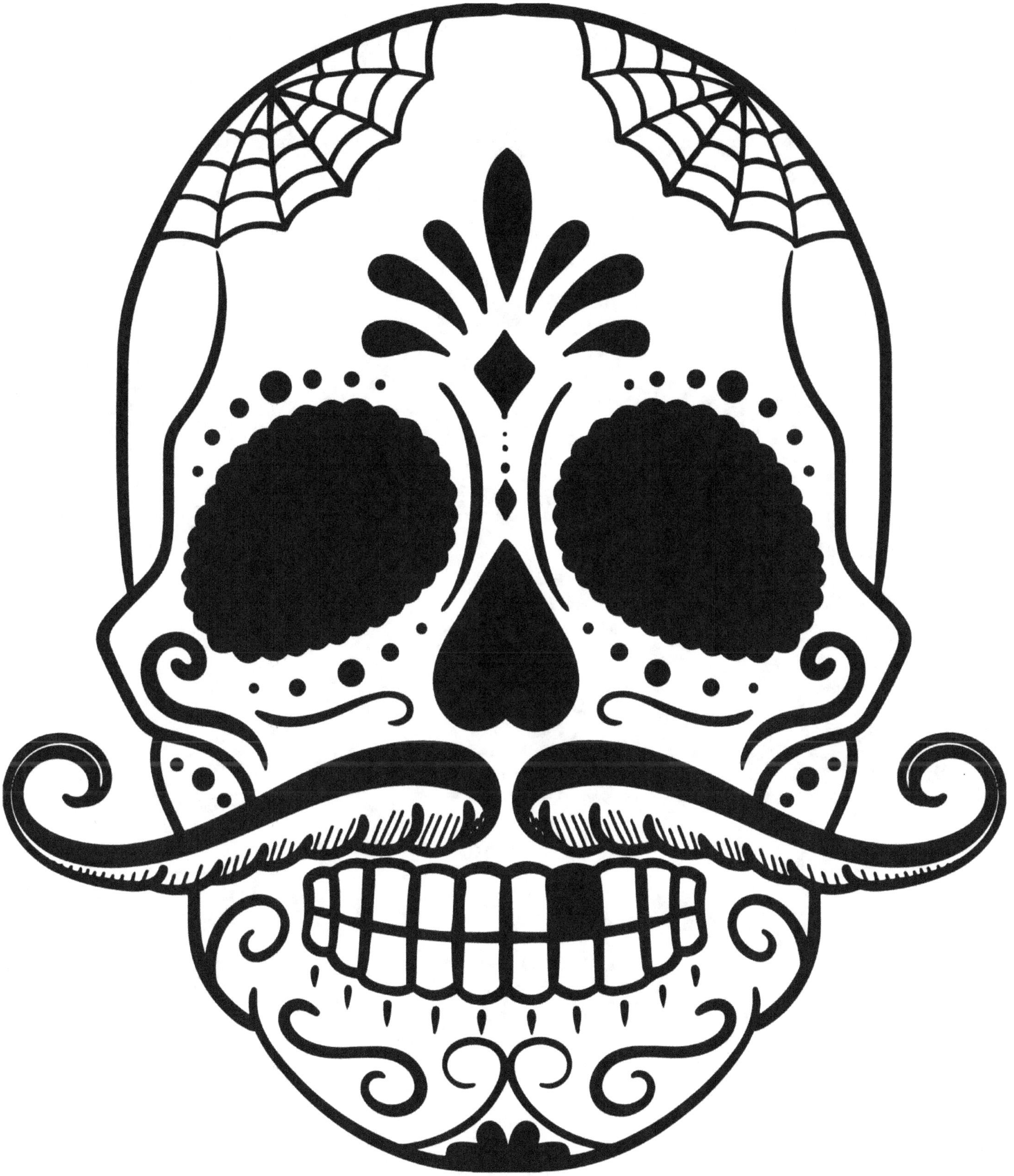

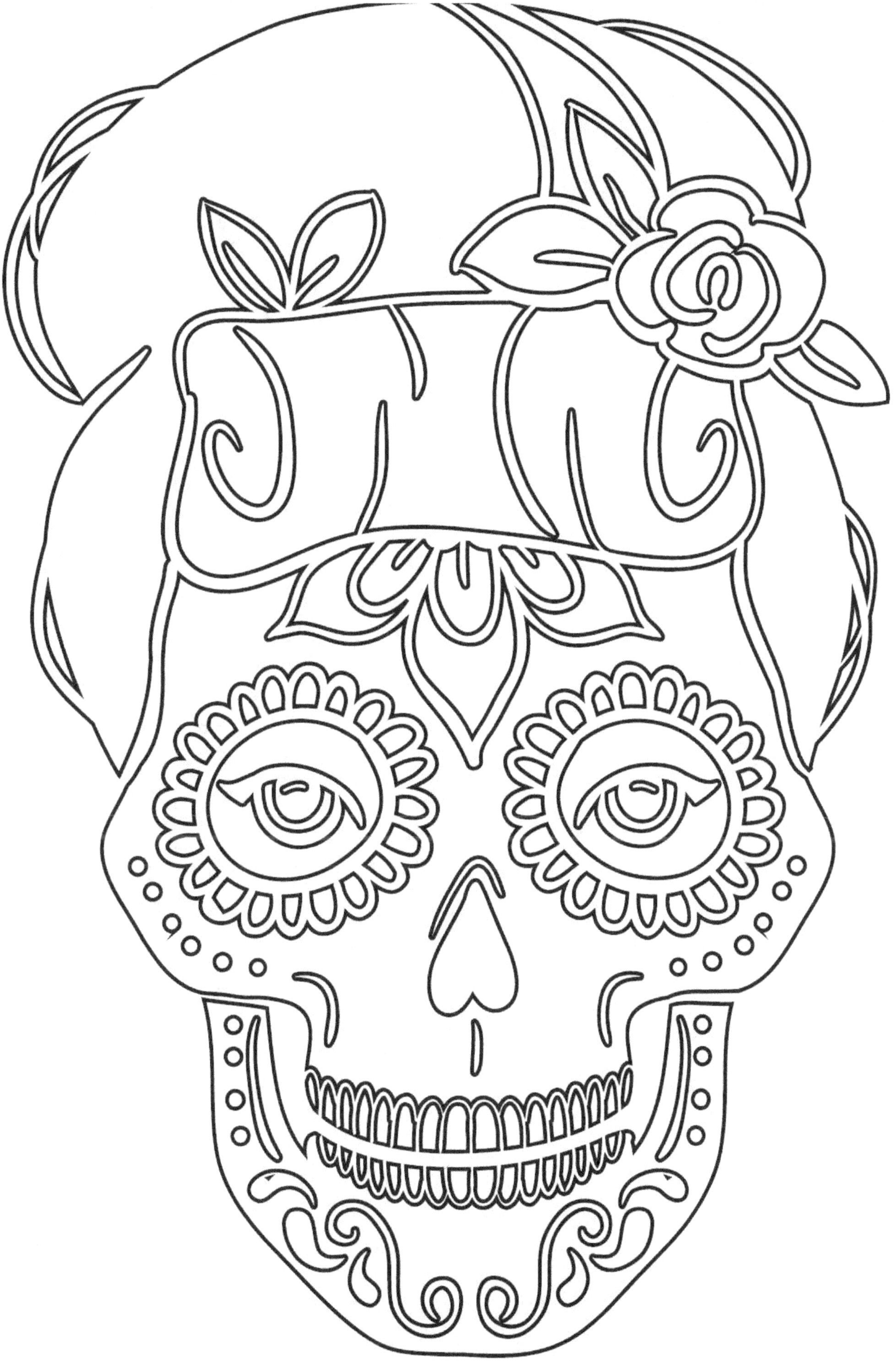

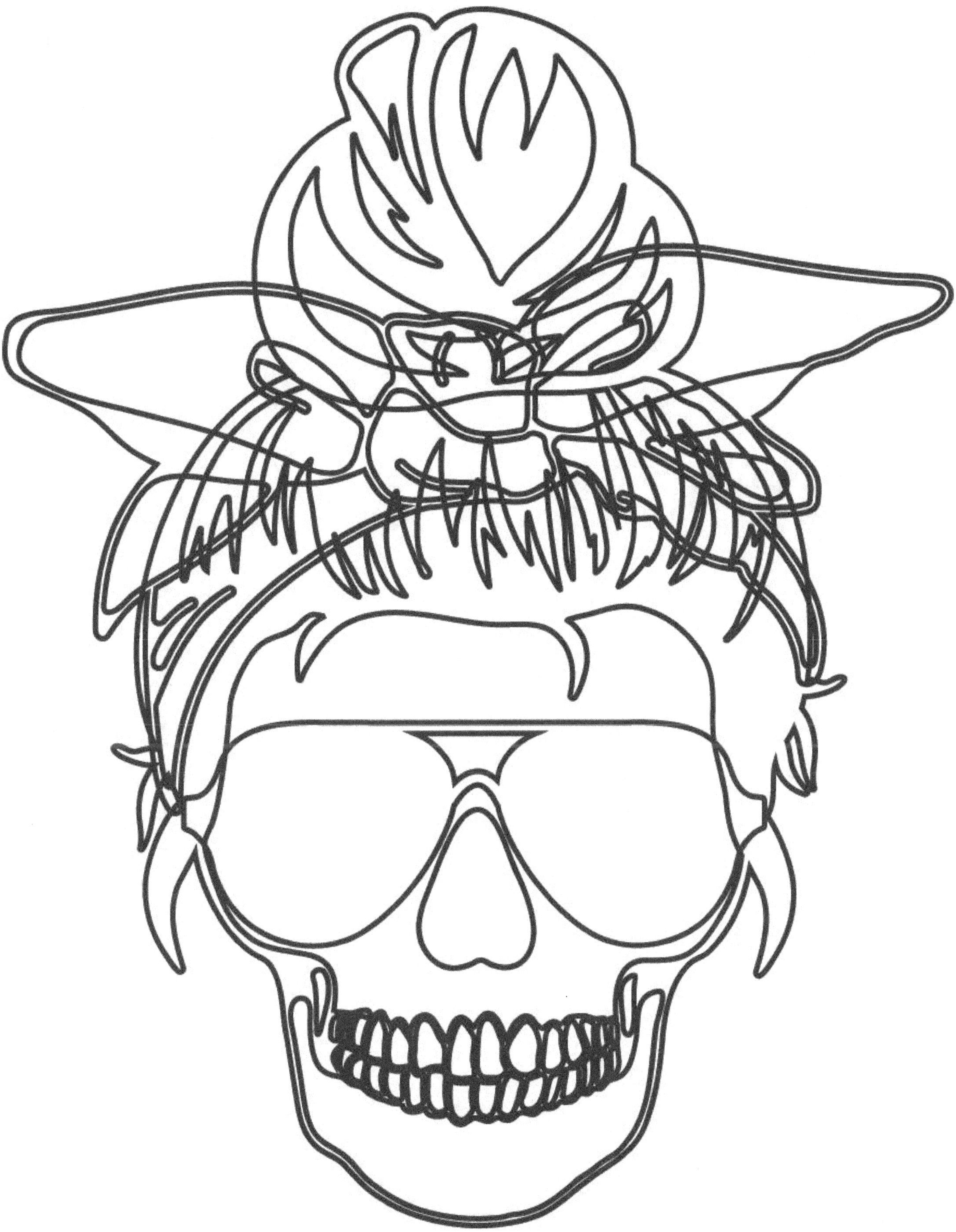

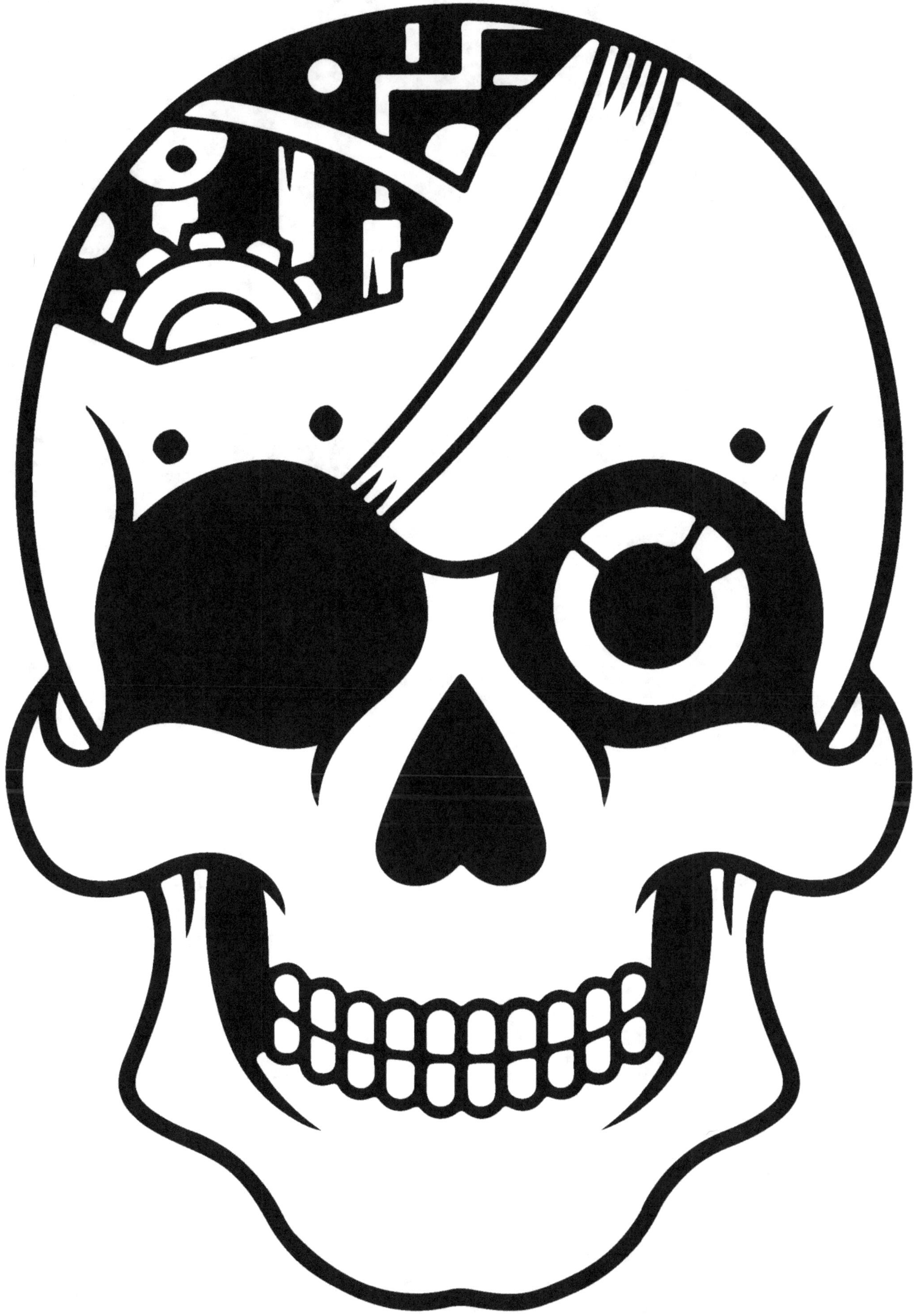

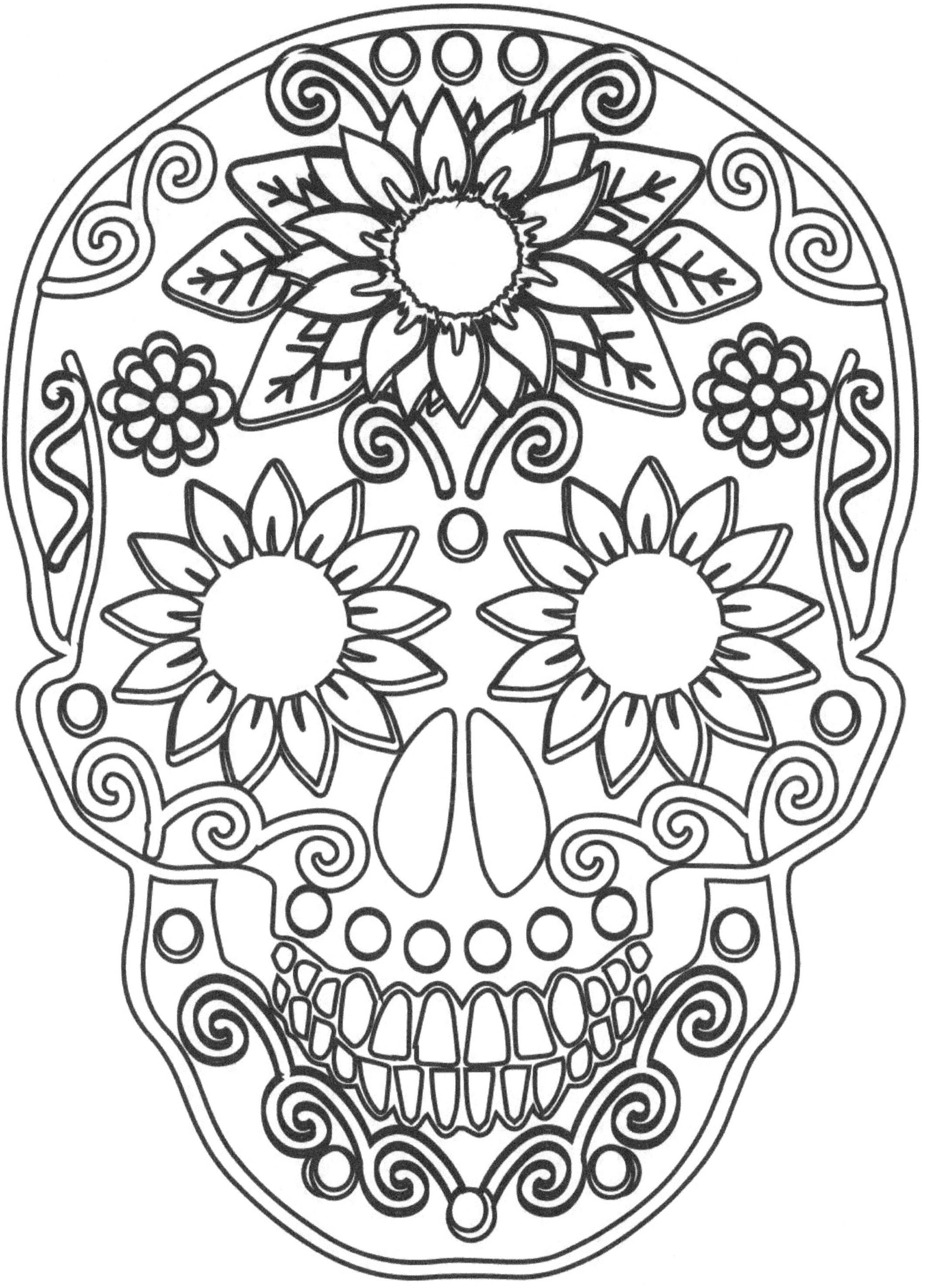

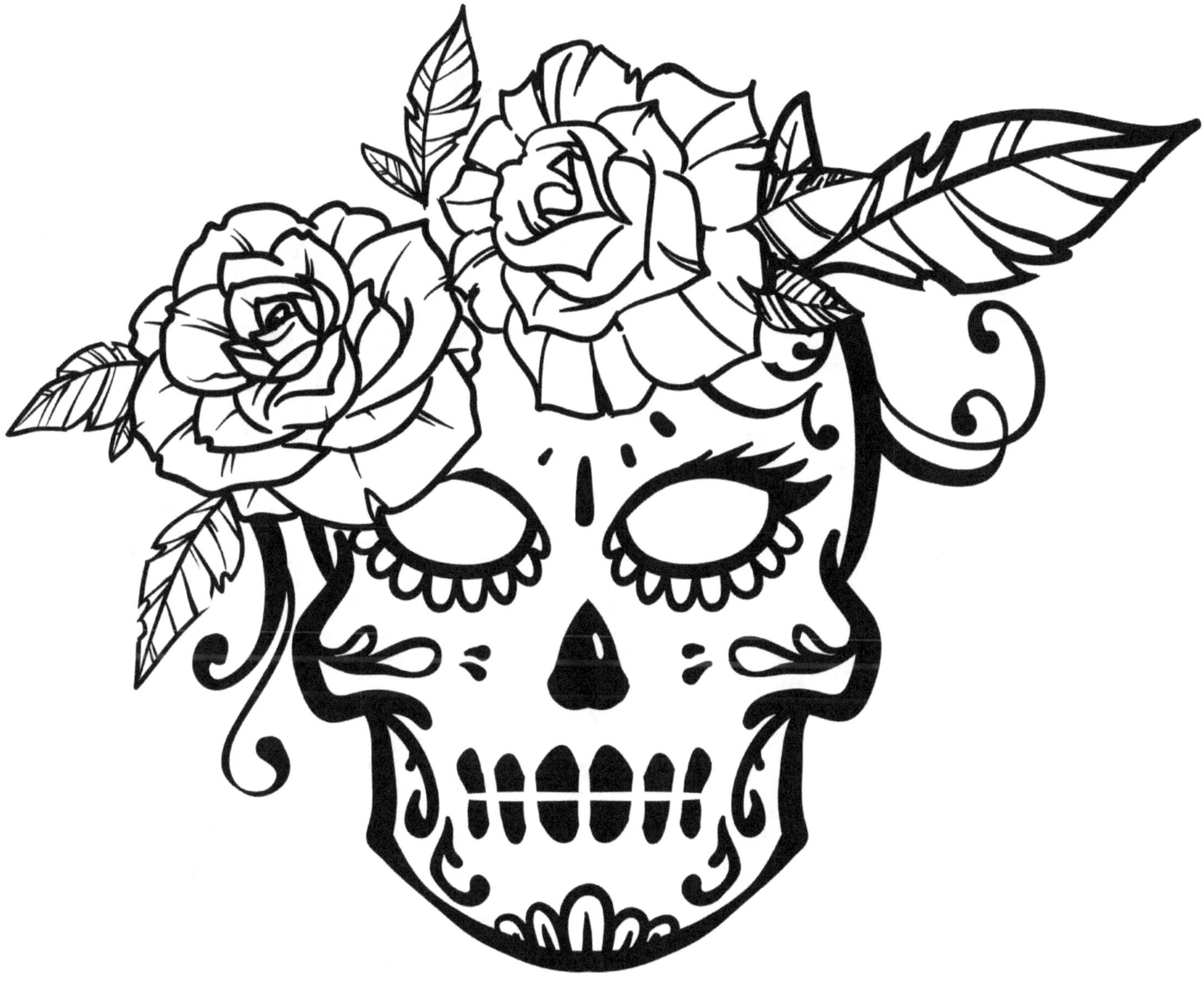

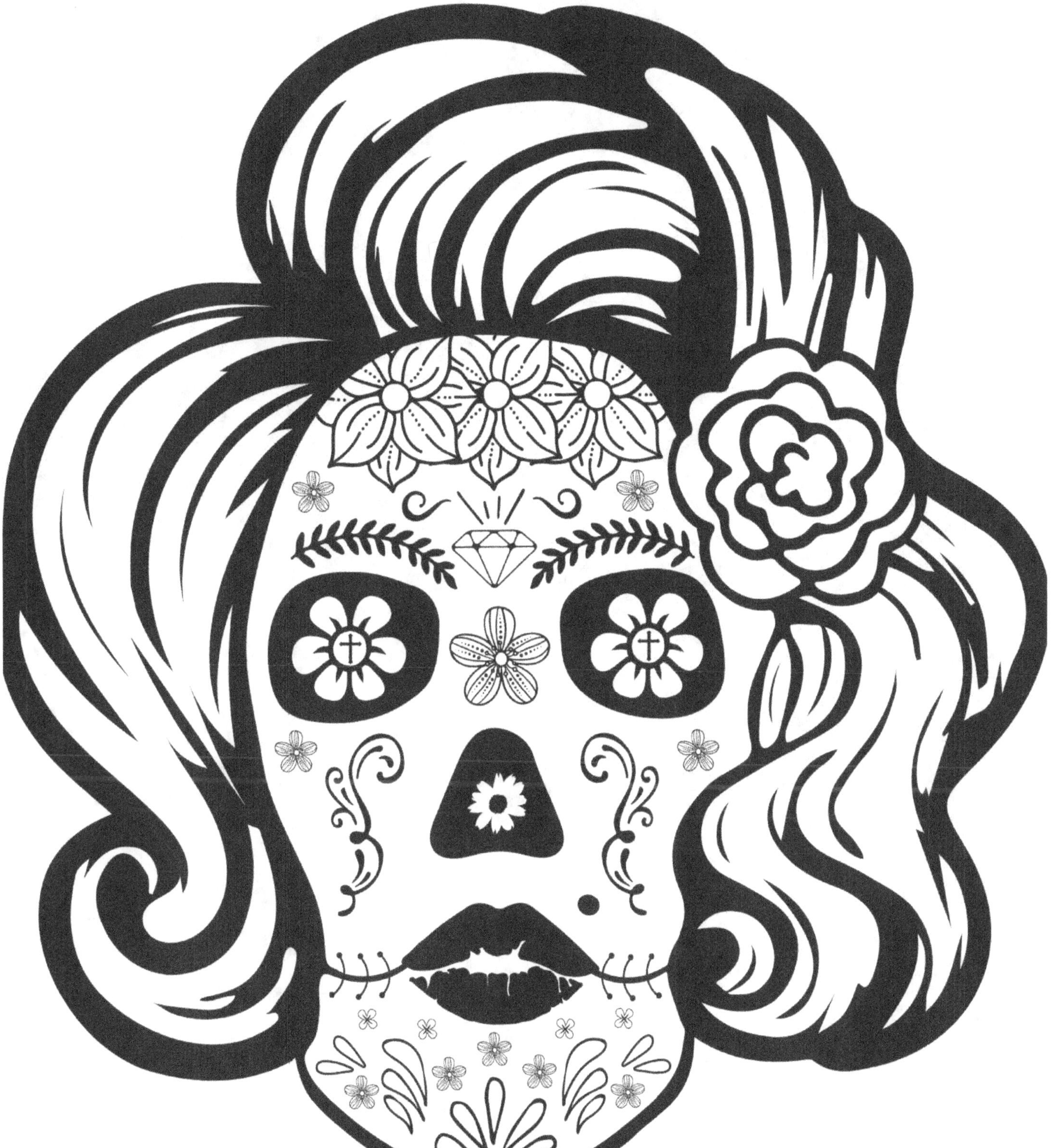

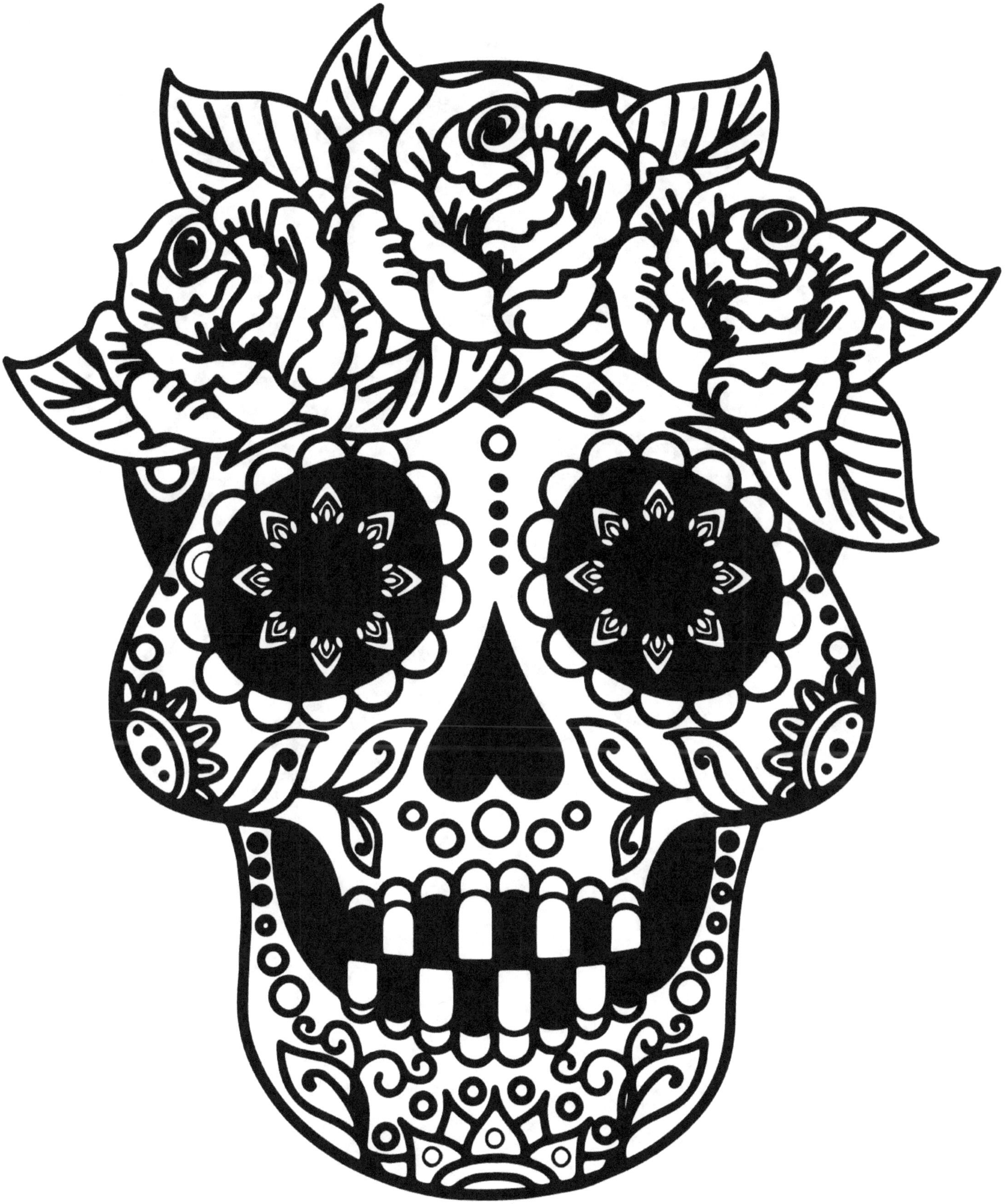

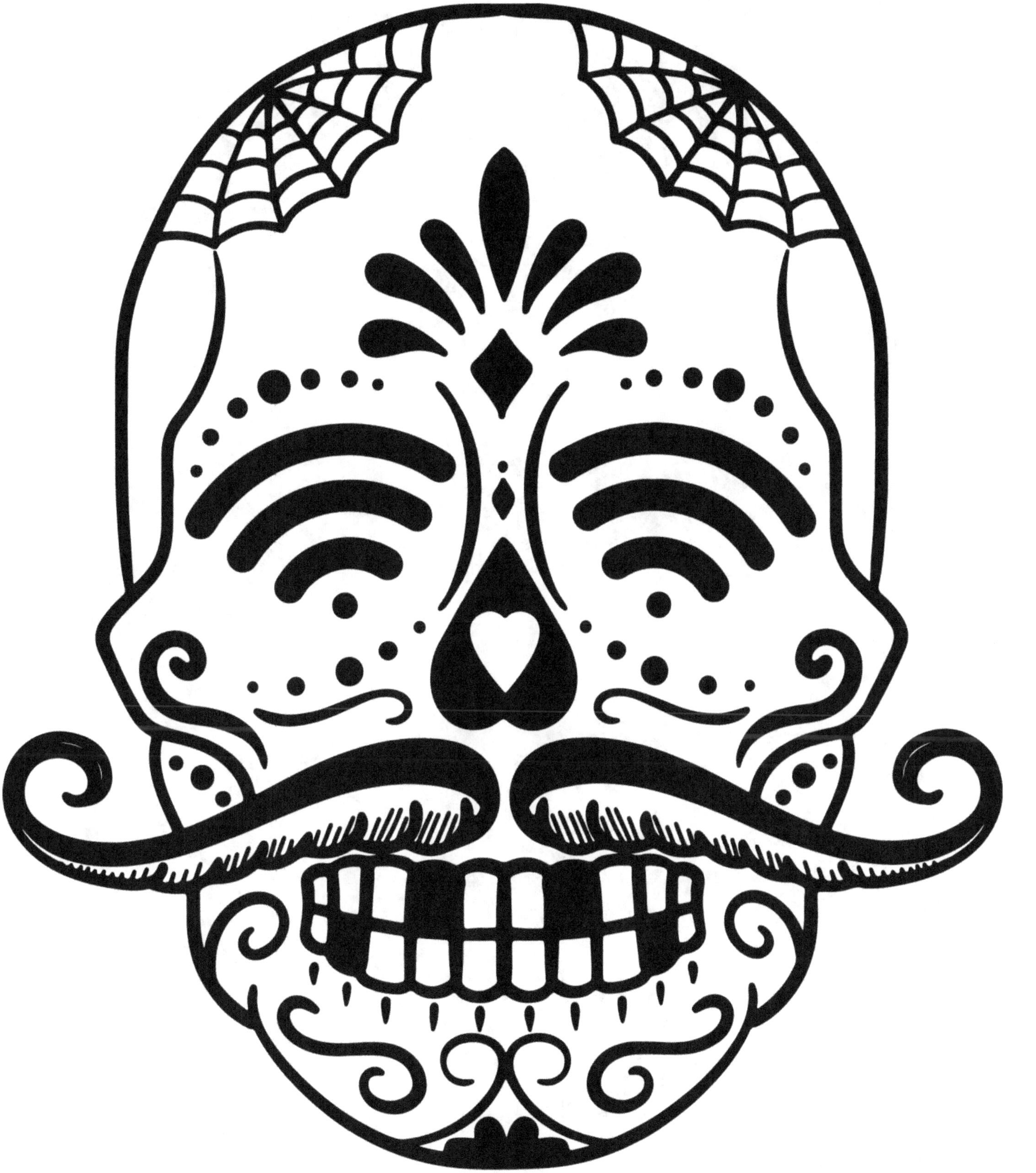

www.ingramcontent.com/pod-product-compliance
Lightning Source LLC
Chambersburg PA
CBHW081519220526
45467CB00010B/2977
* 9 7 9 8 7 0 2 7 5 5 0 8 3 *